D0177750

90710 000 372 940

About the author

Chris England is a sports and comedy writer. His previous work includes the stage plays and subsequent films *An Evening With Gary Lineker* and *Breakfast With Jonny Wilkinson*, and the books *Balham to Bollywood* – a Radio 4 Book of the Week – and *No More Buddha, Only Football*, about the 2002 World Cup. In addition, he has worked on the radio shows 7 Day Sunday and 7 Day Saturday for BBC Radio FiveLive, and contributed to the bestselling Pub Landlord books *The Book of British Common Sense* and *Think Yourself British* with Al Murray, The Pub Landlord. His trilogy of novels about Arthur Dandoe and Charlie Chaplin is published by Old Street.

On the Game

HOW FOOTBALL BECAME
WHAT IT IS TODAY

CHRIS ENGLAND

London Borough of Richmond Upon Thames		
RTTW	DISCARDED	
90710 000 372 940		
Askews & Holts		
796.334 ENG	£7.99	
		9781910400746

Published in Great Britain in 2018 by
Old Street Publishing Ltd
Sulivan Road, London SW6

www.oldstreetpublishing.co.uk

ISBN 978-1-910400-74-6

The right of Chris England to be identified as the author of this work has been asserted by him in accordance with the Copyright, Designs and Patents Act 1988.

Copyright © 2018 by Chris England

All rights reserved. No part of this publication may be reproduced,

stored in or introduced into a retrieval system, or transmitted, in any form, or by any means (electronic, mechanical, photocopying, recording or otherwise) without the prior written permission of the publisher.

10 9 8 7 6 5 4 3 2 1

A CIP catalogue record for this title is available from the British Library.

Printed and bound by CPI Group (UK) Ltd, Croydon, CR0 4YY

Contents

Introduction

In my kitchen drawer I have a novelty bottle opener from 1996 that plays a tinny electronic version of *Three Lions* every time I use it to open a bottle of beer. As a result, that infuriatingly hooky 'Football's Coming Home' riff has accompanied all my attempts to absorb the 22 years of further hurt that have come along since, and now it makes me salivate like Pavlov's alcoholic dog.

As you can imagine, then, England's progress through the knockout rounds of the recent world cup in Russia had a profoundly moving effect on me, as it seemingly did on everyone from Cheshire-Cat-grinning Alan Shearer through members of the royal family, via ITV's roster of not-at-all-football-related celebrities to crowds of fans throwing plastic beer glasses into the air as Slabhead Maguire attacked another corner. Everyone, *everyone* was singing that hook again with glee, with hope, with joy.

It wasn't just that my subconscious beer-trigger was being repeatedly pulled. For I am a member of that accursed generation that is just too young to have seen England win the World Cup. None of the glory, just all the crap that came after. All of it. We should have a T-shirt or something.

In the years since England's triumph I have developed memories of that momentous July day in brilliant Technicolor. The thrilling redness of the shirts, the dazzling gold of the Jules Rimet trophy clutched in Bobby Moore's hand, the captain looking cool and dignified despite being perched on his exhausted teammates' shoulders. The white twin towers against the bright blue sunlit sky, the green of the hallowed turf, the jet black of the Russian linesman's shirt, the orange of Alan Ball's hair. Of course, what I'm remembering is the process of the event's rise to mythical status rather than the thing itself, but these are the images that permeated the football that I became enchanted by, absorbed by, obsessed with, as I grew up.

In retrospect, 1966 seems like English football's matchless peak, a high watermark that we can only dream of reaching again, but it didn't feel like that in the years that followed. It felt like the start of a plateau, of a whole era of gleaming rightness.

Baddiel and Skinner had it wrong in 1996. Not thirty years of hurt. Four years of sunlit smugness and certainty, followed by *twenty-six years of hurt*, that's what we'd had up to that point. It would have messed up the scansion of their catchy charttopper, but nobody said the truth was supposed to be easy.

England were the best team in the world, and English football was the best football in the world, that was what it felt like. We lost to Scotland in 1967 – so what? We were world champions. We lost to Yugoslavia in the semi-final of the European Championships in 1968 – so what? We were world champions.

Back then the English league was won by a different team every year – Liverpool, Manchester United, Manchester

City, Leeds, Everton, Arsenal, Derby. These triumphs were orchestrated by such giants as Bill Shankly, Matt Busby, Don Revie and the upstart Brian Clough, who was surely destined to be England manager one day. Although, naturally, Alf Ramsey would have that job for as long as he wanted it, with his bright blue tracksuit and the clipped tones that made him sound like he'd just stepped out of *The Dambusters*.

As the 1970 World Cup approached, there was great confidence that England could retain the trophy in Mexico. Most of the Boys of '66 were still in the squad. We may have lost the full backs, Cohen and Wilson, but Newton and Cooper were even better, and we had Alan Mullery and Colin Bell now. Pelé, Jairzinho, Beckenbauer, Muller, Mazzola, Rivera – all great players, no doubt, but so what? We were world champions.

And then we weren't.

In the half century that has passed since England were indisputably the best, the game that I fell in love with has seen a multitude of changes on and off the field, inside and outside the stadia, in the rulebook, in how it is presented on the television, and in the incredible oceans of cash that are swilling about, and I think I'd be lying if I said that all of those changes were changes for the better.

I tend to characterise my relationship with football nowadays as a love-hate one. There is much to dislike, but I can't take my eyes off it. But I was hooked at an early age, and my fate was sealed then. I wonder whether today's young people are as captivated as I once was, now that the gulf between players and public is bigger than ever, now that our status on the world stage is eroded every time we head to an international tournament, and now that the game's sheer ubiquity makes it paradoxically easier to ignore. At bottom, though, it's still the same game, still eleven men against eleven, booting an inflatable sphere around a bright green sward, even if the playing field is in many ways less even than it has ever been.

So let's take a look at some of those myriad changes, shall we, and see what we make of them all?

On
The Toss of a Coin

Let's start with the World Cup final of 1966. If England were to find themselves pitted against Germany in the knockout stages of a tournament nowadays, two panicky thoughts would instantly flit across the synapses of every England supporter. First that the Germans are our nemesis, our bogey team, and second, this: 'Oh God, I hope it doesn't go to penalties!'

Back in 1966, however, neither of those things would have occurred to anyone. Our record against the Germans – the West Germans – before the final was: Played 7 Won 6 Drawn 1 Lost 0. We'd beaten them in a friendly only a few months earlier, with Nobby Stiles scoring the only goal of the game. If anything, we were *their* bogey team.

And, as the England fans were shortly to celebrate in song, we had a pretty good record against them in World Wars. The fact that Alf Ramsey sounded like Guy Gibson out of *The Dambusters* could only have added to German apprehension.

As for the penalty anxiety: let us consider what would have

happened if Tofik Bakhramov, the Russian[1] linesman, had disallowed England's third goal. Looking at what footage there is as dispassionately as possible, one can only say that Geoff Hurst's assertion that the ball was a metre over the line suggests a very poor grasp of the metric system.

Suppose, then, that extra time had concluded with no further scoring, and no people on the pitch. Would the (West) Germans have then been able to demonstrate their steely superiority from the penalty spot? Well, no they wouldn't, because the penalty shoot-out hadn't been introduced at that time. If the game had finished all square then there would have been a replay on the Tuesday evening at Wembley – always presuming that there hadn't been some sort of double booking with the greyhound racing. And if that second game had also finished level then the World Cup would have been decided by the toss of a coin.

Imagine that, either way. Bobby Moore calls correctly, and Wembley erupts into joyous celebration. Probably some people would have run onto the pitch while the coin was still spinning in mid-air, thinking it was all over, but then the coin would have slapped onto the back of referee Dienst's hand, he would have indicated a home triumph, and bells would have rung out across the land. Or: Uwe Seeler guesses right, and he and his colleagues begin their uber-efficient celebration of a second World Cup, while the stunned home crowd troops slowly out of Wembley stadium, having the first of what would doubtless have been many bitter conversations about how the Germans were really good at the coin toss, how we should have practised it more in training, and how that disallowed Hurst goal was

---

1 He was actually from what is now Azerbaijan.

definitely over the line, perhaps not a metre over, but still. And decades of inferiority complex would have begun, in the belief that our football team was inherently cursed.

We don't have to imagine it because at the very next tournament, the European Championships of 1968, the semi-final in Naples saw the home team take on Russia. The Italians were anxious about playing the Russians, who had knocked them out of the previous two tournaments, and that fact coupled with their innate caution meant that the match had nil-nil written all over it.

And so, with a place in the final at stake, the Italian captain, Giacinto Facchetti, and his Russian counterpart, Albert Shesternev, were called upon to decide the outcome by a coin toss.

'I went up with the Russian captain,' said Facchetti. 'We went down to the dressing rooms together, accompanied by two administrators from the two teams. The referee pulled out an old coin and I called tails. It was the right call and Italy were through to the final. I went racing upstairs as the stadium was still full and about 70,000 fans were waiting to hear the result. My celebrations told them that they could celebrate an Italian victory.'

Other clues were Shesternev pulling out of the car park in a brand new Ferrari, and the referee trying manfully to remove a horse's head from his kitbag.

The extraordinary thing is that the coin toss took place behind closed doors. Imagine the fuss Sky would make of that nowadays. Or even the BBC, who now have that half-hour programme on BBC2 for the FA Cup draw with fans standing around waiting to hear their team's name so they can make that strange lowing noise they make which only sounds like a cheer if there are a lot more people doing it. There could have been extended post-match punditry, with Alan Shearer saying: 'It was a great opportunity, but he really should'a gone "heads"'

The final of the 1968 European championship saw Italy play Yugoslavia, who had knocked out England in the semi. There was provision for a replay, which Italy won, but clearly something needed to be done. And so it was. By the time the next World Cup came along there would be penalty shoot-outs to decide drawn knockout games.

If coin tosses had been used for the last half-century, England surely couldn't have fared as badly as they have from twelve yards. As for Germany, the laws of chance suggest that they would have lost half the ones they've won. The whole landscape of international football might have been different. Not to mention the sporting psyches of both nations.

Bring back the coin toss, I say. Let's give ourselves a sporting chance.

On
Mexico 1970

If you have fallen under football's spell, then World Cups are the staging posts of your life. The Euros are a kind of holding pattern, filling in the even numbered years while we are waiting for the next World Cup to come along. Euro 96, of course, was a big one, both because it was played in England, and because we hadn't qualified for the 1994 World Cup. By and large, though, it is the World Cups that burn themselves indelibly onto your memory's retina.

Mexico 1970 was my first one. I had the Panini stickers, and the little plasticky Esso coin collection, and a little booklet that came free with Wizard called *The Team That Won the World Cup*, all about 1966. On the cover there was a picture of Jackie Charlton looking over at Ray Wilson, who had the Jules Rimet trophy on his head. Thrillingly for child me, Ray Wilson, by 1970, was an Oldham Athletic player, if no longer an England one.

Hot and high up
This World Cup was like an impossibly exotic dream, compared

to the mud-spattered hackfests of the domestic league. It was the first to be broadcast in colour, an innovation England marked by playing in all-white. And for the first time at a World Cup tournament the alien conditions were a real factor. The ferocious heat of the Mexican summer, coupled with the effects of playing at altitude, dictated the style of the matches. Stamina was at a premium, and the good old bull-in-a-china-shop stuff was out if you wanted to last a whole game.

Demonstrating the blithe disregard for the well-being of players and supporters that was to become their trademark, FIFA decreed that games would kick off at midday, in 98 degree heat, to fit in with European television schedules i.e. so as not to clash with *On The Buses*.

Brazil gave themselves three whole months of preparation, getting used to the altitude, getting used to the heat, becoming a team. They were playing friendlies together, sometimes two a week, from the beginning of March onwards.

England's brief acclimatisation, by contrast, was a friendly in Colombia, where they became embroiled in an extraordinary distraction when captain Bobby Moore was accused of stealing a necklace from a jeweller's in a hotel.

The European teams, as they still do, played their league seasons right up to the time the national teams got together to head to Mexico. Nowadays this affects the Brazilians' build-up too, since most of them have chased the money to Europe, to Spain, to Italy, to England and to Russia. Back in 1970, though, all 22 Brazilians played their football in Brazil. Indeed there were only nine players across all sixteen squads who plied their trade outside their home country. Six of these were Swedes, of whom three played in Belgium, as did the single ex-pat Czech and all 22 Belgians, which meant that the Belgian League was the most heavily represented. I'm pretty sure that's not happening again any time soon.

Fun in the sun

Right from the start England were the moustache-twirling pantomime villains of the piece. Alf Ramsey took along 140lb of beefburgers, 400lb of sausages, 300lb of frozen fish and ten cases of tomato ketchup, demonstrating a lack of trust in the host country's cuisine that would almost certainly be enough to get Gareth Southgate the sack in these hyper-sensitive days.

After a dehydrating 1-0 win over Romania in the opening game, England faced Brazil in Guadalajara's Jalisco Stadium in a Group 3 match that many thought would be replayed further down the line as the final.

Images of the occasion are seared on my brain to this day by the bright Mexican midday sun. Pelé leaping to plant a seemingly perfect header into the bottom corner, Gordon Banks scrambling across to flick it up and over at the last impossible instant. Bobby Moore tracking Jairzinho into the area and picking his pocket with the most immaculately timed tackle you will ever see. (How he spent four days in jail for nicking a necklace is beyond me – if he'd wanted to nick it there's no way he wouldn't have got away with it.) Pelé receiving a cross from Tostão, and just pausing for a moment where any other forward in the history of the game would surely have rushed, before rolling the ball to his right for the onrushing Jairzinho to smash in the game's only goal. And England's chances to equalise: Jeff Astle, added to the squad to bolster the baritone section on *Back Home*, shanking a good chance wide from about ten yards, and Alan Ball, who was responsible for hitting most of the high notes, hitting the bar with a header.

And finally, Pelé and Bobby Moore, shirtless and exhausted, embracing one another with warm smiles of friendship and mutual respect, looking forward to meeting again in a couple of weeks' time at the Estadio Azteca, whereas in fact they would next meet on the set of *Escape to Victory*. Because Ramsey's men progressed to a quarter-final showdown with West Germany, after sleepless nights thanks to malevolent Mexican car horns outside their hotel windows and an unhealthy surfeit of sausages and ketchup.

Back home

Who's to say Ramsey was wrong to bring his own barbecue fixings, though, because ultimately it was food poisoning that undid England. Gordon Banks was generally acclaimed as the best goalkeeper in the world, but when he was struck down by Montezuma's Revenge he was forced to sit out the crucial quarter-final against West Germany. And when I say he sat it out, I mean he spent most of it on the bog. Just so we're clear.

Peter Bonetti took over, and made a name for himself by diving over a Beckenbauer daisy-cutter, flailing under a Seeler back header, and staring like a rabbit caught in some headlights as Muller volleyed in from about a foot out. England, from 2-0 up, and with Bobby Charlton sitting out the last twenty minutes to save him for the semi, lost 3-2, and the rest of the tournament belonged to Brazil.

Meanwhile Gordon Banks had been watching – on and off – back at the team hotel and the broadcast had a delay on it, so when his team mates returned, despondent and dejected, he still thought it was 2-0 and that they were winding him up.

Even though it was bitterly disappointing, Mexico 70 was magical. Even though England were no longer world champions. Even though it was the start of an inferiority complex against both Brazil and the Germans that has us in its evil grasp to this day. Even though PM Harold Wilson was so sure of England's progress that he called a general election during the tournament, counting on a feelgood factor that vaporised in the Mexican heat – meaning that it led directly to the Tory government which took us into the Common Market and ultimately Thatcherism.

Despite all that, Mexico 70 remains the one to beat.

On
The 1970 Brazil Team

If you're going to set your stall out (a phrase only used by costermongers and football pundits) as the best football team the world has ever seen, then you might as well start by getting yourself the best ever football kit. Brazil adopted the yellow shirts and blue shorts after their disastrous 1950 tournament on home soil, when they lost to Uruguay. Up to that point they had always played in all-white, but so traumatic was the *Maracanazo*, the nickname they gave to that national tragedy, that they wanted to draw a line under it forever and start again. And in 1970 the yellow shirt with green trim – no maker's logo, no sponsor – became the most iconic top in football history.

Even though they had won two of the previous three tournaments, Brazil were not the favourites for the 1970 World Cup, not even at home. There was still great dissatisfaction with the team's performance in England in 1966, where they fell foul of what Carlos Alberto politely described as the 'power football' played by the European teams. In effect Pelé was kicked out of the competition, first by the Bulgarians and then the Portuguese.

Their coach for the qualifiers – an unfamiliar indignity for their fans – was João Saldanha. He was a journalist, abrasive, opinionated and unpopular. Imagine that, when Arsene Wenger left, instead of Unai Emery Arsenal had appointed Piers Morgan – that wouldn't have gone down well, would it? As if that wasn't enough, when he was publicly criticised by the coach of Flamengo, Saldanha pulled a gun on him.

Plenty of Brazilians reckoned an ex-footballer – or at the very least some sort of football coach – should be in charge of the Seleção, including the President of the Republic, General Emilio Medici. He was far from impressed with the fact that Saldanha was a communist, having recently overthrown the previous president whilst accusing him of trying to turn Brazil into a communist state. Like many Brazilians, Medici was also agitated that Saldanha didn't think Tostão and Pelé could play together, and that he had proposed dropping Pelé because of his poor eyesight.

Nonetheless, Saldanha won every game in qualifying for Mexico, so just imagine how blinking unpopular he must have been to be sacked.

The Trick of the Five Number 10s

His replacement, Mario Zagalo, had played in the winning teams of 1958 and 1962, and he was the antidote to the opinionated Saldanha. He listened to everybody. He listened to public opinion, he listened to his senior players, and he listened to the president, who wanted him to pick the fabulously-monickered Dadá Maravilha (Wonder Dad).

Never mind about only having room for one of Tostão and Pelé, Zagalo built his team around no fewer than five players who were the regular number tens for their clubs – and back then being the number ten meant you really were the main man. There was Pelé, the actual number ten, there was Tostão, and there was Gérson, Rivelino and Jairzinho.

Remember how much trouble we had getting Steven Gerrard and Frank Lampard in the same team? And that's without even mentioning Paul Scholes.

It worked, though. All five of their brilliant playmakers scored goals in Mexico. Pelé scored four, Rivelino the free kick master three, Tostão a couple, and Gérson grabbed one in the final. Jairzinho scored in every game, and remains the only player ever to achieve this feat.

They let in goals at the other end as well – only England failed to notch against them – but they always seemed like they were going to be able to score at least one more than you.

Zagalo's men steam-rollered their way past the holders, and gained a measure of revenge for the *Maracanazo* by stuffing Uruguay 3-1 in the semi-final. The final, and their ultimate rise to the very pinnacle, awaited.

The Final

Their opponents seemed set to give them a real test. The Italians, though they were still recovering from their epic semi-final triumph over West Germany, represented the best defence that Europe had to offer. That semi, dubbed the Game of the Century, had been 1-0 in the 89th minute when Karl-Heinz Schnellinger equalised, leading to a frantic extra-time in which the lead changed hands back and forth, with Rivera finally clinching a 4-3 win.

A great team needs to lay down a defining performance, one that gathers all the strands of their story together and ties them up with a neat bow, and the final was Brazil's. Pelé opened the scoring with a leaping header that might even have beaten Gordon Banks.

Their questionable defence was breached by Boninsegna to level things at half time. Then a powerful strike by Gérson restored the lead, before Pelé nodded down a chance for Jairzinho to score his inevitable goal. Finally they capped it off with a perfect picture book fourth, a sweeping move down the left leading to Pelé taking a calm casual moment in the box, as he had against England, and then rolling it into the path of the onrushing skipper Carlos Alberto who slammed it low and hard into the corner.

After the game, Tarcisio Burgnich, the Italian tasked with marking Pelé, said: 'I told myself before the game "he's made of skin and bones just like everyone else". But I was wrong.'

Brazil got to keep the Jules Rimet Trophy, as the Italians would have done, for winning it a third time. They didn't get to keep it for long, however, as in 1983 it was stolen. The Brazilian Football Confederation had ordered a replica, but for some reason the replica was in the safe, and the real one was on display in their offices in Rio. It was in a box made of bullet-proof glass, so at least it wasn't going to get shot, but the box was just nailed to the wall. One night some thieves broke in, distracted the one guard, pulled the box off the wall and ran off with it, and the little trophy that Carlos Alberto had raised triumphantly above his head in the Estadio Azteca was melted down and spent.

The more lasting prize his team won in Mexico in 1970, though, was to be acclaimed as the world's best ever team. To this day everyone has a soft spot for Brazil (except the Argentinians), and every Brazilian team since has had great things expected of it, even ones with David Luiz in them. Sometimes they come close, as in the Socrates team of 1982, and sometimes they don't, as when they lost 7-1 to Germany and that bloke in the crowd started eating his shirt. What a shirt, though…

On
Shirts

When I first got into football a team's shirt was quite a simple bit of gear. It was just the colour they wore so you could tell which players were on your team. Some of them, but by no means all, would have a team badge or crest but that would be it. On the back there would be a number from one to eleven that would have told you roughly what position on the field you could expect the wearer to be playing.

If you wanted to show your support for these plain-clad heroes you would buy a scarf in similar colours, or maybe – if you were a bit flash – a silk scarf with the team's name on that you could tie around your wrist. Perhaps you'd have a rosette, or a bobble hat, or a small selection of lapel badges.

Nowadays go to any shopping centre anywhere in the country, not even on a match day, and you will invariably encounter swathes of fat blokes waddling around in hi-tech sweat redistribution systems acting as XXXL billboards for Chinese betting companies.

So when did we start down that particular road? When did

football clubs work out that they could flog the chest space of their loyal fan base, who would pay through the nose for the privilege, over and over again?

The first company to come up with the idea that fans might like to wear the same shirts as the players was Admiral. They'd been making shirts for Don Revie's Leeds, who were certainly interested in exploring ways to sell more merch to their supporters. Remember that badge they brought out where the L and the U were contorted into a smiley? Remember those sock ties they used to wear? With the player's number hanging down the side of the lower leg like a frilly dark blue flag?

Those didn't catch on, but the idea of replica kits did, properly starting with Admiral's revolutionary deal with England when Revie took over there in 1974. The Admiral kit was the first official England shirt to include the manufacturer's logo on the chest, and they paid the Football Association £15,000 for the privilege. The deal also allowed Admiral to sell replica shirts to supporters, which cost £5 – or £9 if you bought shorts and socks as well.

The BBC threatened not to broadcast the 1976 FA Cup Final because both teams were wearing the Admiral logo and it contravened their guidelines on advertising. There were questions in parliament about whether the rise in replica kits was unfairly exploiting children's interest in football.

This commercial distaste was overcome, and soon there were larger issues to deal with. In this country, Southern League Kettering Town were the first to wear shirts with a sponsor's name emblazoned across the chest in 1976. Manager Derek Dougan did a four-figure deal with Kettering Tyres, which brought him an indignant letter from the Football Association ordering him to cease and desist. Dougan brilliantly changed the lettering to Kettering T and claimed it stood for 'town' rather than 'tyres'.

Some countries in Europe – Germany, Austria and Denmark – already allowed shirt sponsorship, and it was quickly seen as a potential source of some much-needed extra revenue for clubs. Despite the misgivings of some, such as Arsenal chairman Peter Hill-Wood, who felt that football clubs 'would be losing a little bit of our identity', shirt sponsorship deals began creeping in. In 1979 Liverpool signed a £100,000 deal with Hitachi, the Japanese electrical giant. Television companies – the BBC anxious about their own sense of identity, ITV worried about losing advertising revenue of their own – refused to show sponsored shirts at first, so Liverpool couldn't wear the new Hitachi shirts in televised domestic or European games.

This niggle was also overcome, and it wasn't long before, for example, Solvite realised that Watford had a similar colour scheme to their packaging, and the Hornets were walking out looking like walking packets of wallpaper paste.

The replica kit industry received a great shot in the arm for the second season of the Premier League, now to be called the Premiership. The traditional 1-11 numbering was to be abandoned, and clubs could use squad numbering and players' names on the backs of their shirts. In no time the club shops had those hot iron presser things, and fans could buy tops with a favourite player's name on, on their own name, or their nickname, or their kid's name, and they could rinse you for the numbers as well.

Never mind that you could no longer really have the pub conversation about who was the best number nine in the league, because he might be wearing number nineteen until the previous number nine moved on to pastures new. For those looking to flog shirts, though, it was boom time, because with names and numbers, every transfer in or out created exciting new replikit sales opportunities.

The shirt sponsorship market boomed – today it is worth £300 million to the Premier League clubs – and the rise of the replica kit was a big part of that. Football fans, it seemed, were quite happy to be turned into walking billboards. Indeed, they would be anxious to have not only the latest kit colour, with the slightly altered neckline and their chosen name and number, but also the up-to-date shirt sponsor on their chest. Even when this was not a particularly positive message to cart around. For a while Oldham were sponsored by our hooky owner's company, and wore the name Torex Foundation on our shirts. It made us look like we were sponsored by some sort of evil criminal conglomerate with sinister aspirations towards global domination – 'They're called the Torex Foundation, Mister Bond, but we know very little about them. Take yourself off to the Caribbean, sleep with a few women, see what you can find out...' That particular owner – Chris Moore, his name was, and I expect he's in jail somewhere – bailed on the club having stripped every asset that wasn't physically nailed down (including, I believe, some nails), and the Torex Foundation shirts were stuck in a bottom drawer never to be seen again. At least they'd been more inspiring than their predecessor, the Slumberland–sponsored kit, which hardly seemed an advert for excitement, but still.

Through the 1980s the large Japanese electrical companies had something of a monopoly across Europe's biggest clubs. Sharp (Manchester United), JVC (Arsenal), Hitachi (Liverpool, Ac Milan, Hamburg) NEC (Everton), TDK (Ajax) and Brother (Manchester City) all took advantage. Later it was beer – Holsten Pils (Spurs) Carlsberg (Liverpool), Shipstones

(Nottingham Forest), McEwans (Blackburn Rovers) Coors (Chelsea) – until the prevailing mood thankfully made this sort of thing something of a taboo.

Then the way was clear for shonky banks like Northern Rock (all the way to its collapse) and unscrupulous money-lenders like Wonga to sponsor high profile clubs like Newcastle United.

After the turn of the millennium football shirts started to reflect the rise of the Middle East as a global financial power zone, with the region's biggest airlines Emirates and Etihad getting into big sponsorship deals, not only shirts but stadia too.

The big trend in recent years has been towards betting companies as shirt sponsors. Anyone can see that football and betting are inextricably linked. Barely an ad break goes by without a giant Ray Winstone looming over a stadium growling 'It's all abaht the in-play!' or bellowing something about how it's time to 'Cash Aht!' Nine of the twenty Premier League clubs – and their many thousands of XXXL walking billboards – now carry sponsorship by betting firms. Bookies are spending more and more on sponsorship because they are themselves a boom business and football is leading their market. Last year British punters lost £14 billion to them, and shirt sponsorship is surely funnelling even more gullible souls towards their sites. Someone worked out (not me) that in an average episode of *Match of the Day* you would see gambling logos or branding 241 times, and they were on screen roughly 30 percent of the time.

The Football Association bans youth teams from wearing gambling logos on their shirts, but shirt sponsorship in televised games is a simple way for betting companies to get around restrictions on advertising to children, and subliminally normalising it as a fun activity.

Such is the global reach of the Premier League that some

of the companies advertising on its tops aren't even aiming at the UK market. Everton are sponsored by Sport Pesa, a betting company based in Nairobi, and Crystal Palace's sponsor this season is Dongqiudi, which is some kind of Chinese football app.

All of which doesn't even get into the smaller local contractors who have taken the opportunity to become sleeve sponsors, or back-of-shorts sponsors, or the bit above the player's name but below the collar sponsors.

What about those sympathetic concerns in parliament back in the 1970s that clubs might rip off their loyal fans and their children? Well, Manchester United's replica kit for the new season costs £183. Make of that what you will.

I have bought replica kits myself, for me and for my three sons, in an attempt to inculcate an attachment to my club while they were at an impressionable age. I don't like to wear them as a casual bit of fashion gear, though – I'm a bit suspicious of exactly where the sweat is being redistributed to by the hi-tech design – but I do wear them to play football in. Apart from the players on the field, though, I don't think anyone looks really good in them. I think they merely highlight the gulf, the aching physical chasm, between the fan and his athletic idol. The older the fan, the more stark this disparity seems. And the more I can't help thinking 'he ought to know better'.

You could hardly ask for a more perfect example of the way football has been prepared to hive off anything it can to commercial interests than to compare some photos of players and crowds from fifty years ago and now. Back then, the plain-shirted lads striving to win for the fans in their lucky scarves; now, the preening fashion icons almost completely camouflaged against the wall of identically-clad replifans.

If that isn't selling your soul I don't know what is.

On
Pelé

Whether or not Pelé was the greatest footballer ever to grace the beautiful game – he is even credited with coining the phrase 'the beautiful game' – he is without doubt its most iconic figure.

He was voted the greatest player of the twentieth century – although actually FIFA had to change the rules of the vote and appoint a panel to decide, because Maradona was galloping away with the internet vote. Mother Nature and Father Time have taken their toll on the numbers of people who can actually claim to have seen Pelé play. And that goes double for the likes of Puskas, Matthews and di Stefano, the greatest players of the previous generation.

Some of Pelé's magic moments are preserved on YouTube, including pretty much all of them from Mexico 1970. Because it was there that he cemented his reputation as the best of the best. The best player, of the best team ever.

Nearly man, nearly...
He was generally already thought of as the world's best in the

1960s, in a rather vague sort of way, but his outrageous scoring feats in South America were a far-off phenomenon. Neither of his chief rivals for the arbitrary title of best player in the world – Eusébio of Portugal and George Best of Northern Ireland – qualified for Mexico 1970, so the stage was set for him to make a lasting statement. Which is what he did.

He'd burst onto the scene in 1958, when his dazzling exploits as a 17-year-old had taken Brazil to their first World Cup. But then a hamstring injury in the first game of the 1962 tournament in Chile side-lined him there as his country picked up a second trophy, and then in 1966 he was kicked from the park by Portugal, and hobbled from the world stage, perhaps, it seemed, for ever. Indeed, he retired from international football after that, and had to be talked into returning for Mexico.

So we could now be talking about Pelé as a footnote, a man who scored an improbable mountain of goals for Santos, but otherwise a former child prodigy who never delivered again when it really mattered. A bit like Wayne Rooney – great at Euro 2004, but then perennially injured or disappointing at tournaments thereafter. Or Paul Gascoigne – brilliant at Italia 90, but subsequently a tearful let-down who ended up managing Kettering for about twenty minutes. Or Michael Owen. Only better.

Mr Ambassador, you are spoiling us...

In his thirties Pelé went to play in America for the New York Cosmos, where his global celebrity was instrumental in setting up one of many attempts to get soccerball started over there where they think they already have football and it's played by blokes in motor cycle helmets. Truth to tell, the standard wasn't that great – Gordon Banks, Pelé's old sparring partner, was

NASL Goalkeeper of the Year even though he had lost an eye in a car accident six years earlier.

For some, Pelé's status as football's number one legend is tarnished by his buddy-buddy relationship with Sepp Blatter, to the point where he might even have been considered a crony. Still, if they will keep inviting him to things he can hardly be blamed for turning up for a free dinner and a wave to the crowd.

And his claim is not burdened by the cheating and the drug abuse that taints Maradona's reputation, or the clouds of tax dodgery and financial chicanery that colour appreciation of Messi and Neymar, nor the preening self-regard that character-ises Cristiano Ronaldo and Zlatan 'I Am Zlatan' Ibrahimovic. Pelé's gentlemanly demeanour has made him an ambassador for the game.

Also for erectile dysfunction, let us not forget that. At the World Cup in Japan every bus stop and tube station wall seemed to have a picture of Pelé on it, giving a cheerful thumbs up, as if tactlessly mocking the afflicted.

Pelé's special skill, as an older gentleman, has been to predict that the nation of whoever he is talking to will win the World Cup, and soon. He didn't really think an African nation was going to win by 2025, he was just talking to some African guy, wasn't sure exactly where he came from, and wanted to make him happy.

The man, the skills...

In the end Pelé's legend rests on some sublime pieces of skill from Mexico 70. Against Czechoslovakia he tried to lob the keeper from the halfway line, missing the goal by a whisker. And against Uruguay he completely bamboozled their hapless custodian with a dummy, running past him, doubling back and firing at the open net, which… well, he missed. Maybe João Saldanha was right about his eyesight.

His trademark move, however, and the one I suspect posterity will recall most fondly, like the Cruyff turn or the Ardiles overhead flick, is his bicycle-stroke-scissors kick goal, a piece of skill so magical that from some angles the ball seems to travel upwards off his boot, while from others it looks like it goes down towards the ground. And the Nazis had deliberately broken his ribs, which made it doubly difficult. It was such a memorable goal that it fully justified his decision not to escape at half time through the tunnel dug by the French Resistance, and even Emperor Ming gave it a standing ovation.

On
Total Football

The 1974 World Cup will always be, for me, the first one that happened in colour. I have seen the colour pictures from Mexico 1970, of course, memorably bright and sun-drenched, most particularly the bright yellow sweat-stained T-shirts of the victorious Brazilians. I have seen also the official film pictures of 1966, and the unforgettable rich red of the shirts worn by Bobby, Bobby and Nobby as they jigged around with the Jules Rimet Trophy perched on one or other of their heads.

Those are after-images, though, hindsight colour, if you like. In real time, live, in my house, it was all still in black-and-white.

The 1974 Mundial in West Germany, though, I watched in colour. I had to go round to a friend's house, or the house of the grandmother of a friend, and watch on my best behaviour, because we didn't get colour until the year after.

And the colour of 1974 was orange.

The brilliant Dutch team captivated the world with their scintillating play, bringing their philosophy of Total Football to the biggest stage.

What it said on the Total Football tin was this: all the players were interchangeable; they were all sufficiently skilful to play in any position. Apart from the goalkeeper, of course, but it was certainly part of the fascination of that Dutch side that the keeper Jongbloed played in the number 8 shirt. In fact, the team in dazzling orange had a relatively conventional formation, with defenders, midfielders and strikers, but they were all given a lot of licence to switch positions as they looked for space to attack, while teammates would be responsible enough and tactically aware enough to cover the positions that had been vacated. They played a high offside line, pressed relentlessly to win the ball back, and swapped positions seamlessly.

Total Football, or something very like it, had been tried before. Hungary's 1950s Golden Team, the Mighty Magyars, had done it, with a deep-lying centre forward called Hidegkuti and the brilliant Ferenc Puskas pulling the strings. Burnley, believe it or not, won the league in 1959-60 with a very similar style. But it was at Ajax Amsterdam in the early 1970s that Total Football began to sweep all before it, as Rinus Michels' team won three European Cups in a row, and the 1974 World Cup was set to be its apotheosis with Michels now at the helm of the national team.

The key to making Total Football work was Johan Cruyff, surely one of the most brilliant footballers ever to play the game. Theoretically at least, Cruyff was the centre forward, but he was anything but a target man. He was the playmaker, roaming all over the opposition half looking for precious space, pulling the defence out of shape. And when he played the ball forward there would be the wide men, Johnny Rep and Robbie Rensenbrinck, charging into the space he had created, or perhaps it would be Johan Neeskens galloping up from midfield, or even Arie Haan, the centre back. It was thrilling stuff.

Holland – for some reason they were always called Holland then, although, as every keen watcher of *QI* knows, Holland is the name of only part of the country, which is properly called the Netherlands – breezed past six opponents in the two-group format that was used back then on their way to the final.

They won them all, apart from a goalless draw against Sweden in which Cruyff unveiled the 'Cruyff turn', feinting to cross with his right foot and instead dragging the ball behind his standing left foot to dart away in the other direction. The hapless Viking defender was left looking this way and that like a character in a Scooby-Doo cartoon, and in every playground of every school in every country of the world the next day kids were trying to emulate this, wrenching knees, jarring hips, crashing to the asphalt with the ball jammed between their ankles (or maybe that was just me).

Holland also dismantled Brazil, the world champions, which felt like a proper passing of the torch from the previous best team in the world. They still had Jairzinho and Rivelino, but in truth the 1974 Brazil side were a shadow of their predecessors without the great Pelé. They were utilitarian, functional and brutish, trying to kick lumps off the Dutch, and their joyless approach had been exemplified by their game with Zaire.

The African newcomers didn't seem too sure of the rules of the game: one of them had sprinted out of a defensive wall to boot the ball away before a free kick could be taken. Yugoslavia had beaten them 9-0, and fans of one-sided blood sports everywhere licked their lips as they lined up against the holders. All Brazil needed to do was win 3-0 to finish ahead of Scotland on goal difference, after two miserably uninspiring goalless draws, and that is all they did, to a collective sigh which nowadays would be summed up with the not-real-word 'Meh...'

Holland arrived at the Olympiastadion in Munich for the final against the hosts, West Germany, seemingly ready to be crowned the best in the world. And it started brilliantly. Jack Taylor – England's only representative at the tournament following Ramsey's team's failure to qualify ahead of Poland, who would finish third – blew his whistle, and the first time a German touched the ball it was to pick it out of the net. Forty-five seconds of fluent ball retention culminated in Cruyff surging into the area and being hacked down, whereupon Johan Neeskens dispatched the penalty.

The stage was set for a real statement, with the additional cake-icing of watching the Germans floundering and humiliated, but somehow it just didn't happen. The Dutch were content to keep the ball, passing it comfortably around with their opponents flailing in their wake, and it seemed as though this was going to be enough for them. Perhaps the animosity left over from the war, only a generation earlier, meant that this mocking, effortless superiority was even more delicious than a thumping win.

As the game wore on, however, the extra few percent of adrenalin provided by the 75,000 strong home crowd began to kick in, and the Germans levelled from the spot, and then went ahead through Gerd Muller just before half time. Helmut Schoen, the German manager, managed to neutralise Cruyff by using full-back Berti Vogts as a man-marker, which took away his ability to draw centre backs out of position and create space. He did generate one great chance, which was fluffed by Rensenbrinck – whom my father would always refer to as Rent-a-brick, much as he always referred to Trevor Cherry as Cherald, 'to give him his full name'.

And then it was over, and the Germans had won. The brilliant orange succumbed to the monochrome Mannschaft, which was really depressing. Football will do that to you, kids.

Like the Mighty Magyars in 1954, and Michel Platini's brilliant French side of 1982, Cruyff and co. were ultimately denied the top step on the podium by the relentless efficiency of the Germans – who, by the way, had also cracked Puskas's ankle in the group stage in 1954, and profited from Harald Schumacher's astonishing unpunished assault on Patrick Battiston in 1982 (see p.52). They really are every neutral's favourites.

On
Matchday Programmes

Further erosion of the olde tyme football experience is apparently imminent after the decision taken at the annual EFL meeting in June 2018 to scrap the requirement for clubs to produce a matchday programme.

I hadn't realised that clubs were obliged to do it, I presumed that it must make sound commercial sense to charge fans three quid or more, the price your local supermarket will charge you for a thriller that would take a week to read and be a damned sight more entertaining, for the statutory glossy pamphlet.

Time was when you needed to pick up a programme to know who was in the team, but the days when people turned to the programme for that information are long gone. Now you get the team news on Twitter before you even get to the game, and you can already have spouted your disrespect for the selection all over the internet.

You used to need a programme to decipher the half time scoreboard, so that you would know which match was referred to by the big capital letters, and whether the scores placed alongside with aching slowness by a bloke up a stepladder were surprising, predictable, irritating or irrelevant to your sense of well-being. Now, of course, you can get the up-to-the-minute scores on your phone, and you're probably keeping an eye on the Ray Winstone community to decide whether or not to 'Cash Aht!'

Maybe you want to read the manager's message to the fans, about how the defeat in midweek was a setback, but the lads are all going to pull together, and it's a marathon not a sprint... but you can see that on the club website, probably, even if the proof-reading has clearly been done by a twelve-year-old and contains numerous examples of phrases like 'we would of liked to of got something down their at there place, but it wasent to be'.

To produce something so overpriced and under-informative is, as usual, indicative of a certain attitude towards supporters – that they are just there so that their arcane habits can be milked. They are probably not quite as bad, in that regard, as the old Premium phone lines; '0898 12 11 42. Welcome to... Latics Clubcall... all the latest news... from Boundary Park... 24 hours a day... seven... days a week...' Those 'pay pauses' (as Harold Pinter used to call his when he was paid by the minute) are strongly reminiscent of a goalkeeper's reluctance to punt a goal kick back into play in the last minute, when the team are sitting on an undeserved point. At least the programme remains (technically) a collectable for your money.

I pretty much decided a few years ago that I didn't need to bother with a programme most of the time, but now that they are to be withdrawn I feel inexplicably miffed about it. Still, that feeling, the inexplicable miffedness – that's what football is all about.

On
Fate Tempting
and Argentina 1978

As flies to wanton boys are we to th' gods.
They kill us for their sport.

Thus William Shakespeare mused on the life of a football fan, tossed, tormented and swatted by the giant hand of Fate. And if there's one thing we know about Fate, it is that she must not be tempted. When a big game is in the offing no pavement crack should be trodden upon, no single magpie can go unsaluted, and – most importantly of all – no outcome can be taken for granted.

Commentators should know this, of course, but even as they banter with one another about 'the curse of the commentator', deep down they cannot stop themselves from tempting Fate.

Most egregiously, during the recent Russian razzmatazz, the commentator for the crucial Germany-Sweden group clash (he shall remain nameless) couldn't contain his glee, never mind retain his balance and his objectivity, as he spent the last twenty minutes screaming stuff like: 'This WILL be the first time Germany have ever failed to win either of their first two group games!' And 'the holders WILL be heading home!'

WILL, WILL, WILL!

Not a conditional tense in sight (or earshot, strictly speaking). Of course, the Germans then equalised with seconds to go. Of course they did, and it was this guy's fault for tempting Fate so damned hard. Never mind that the Swedish keeper was slightly out of position, or that he should have had more men in the wall. It was the commentator what did it – and he then had the sheer unmitigated gall to cry: 'NEVER write off the Germans!'

Until the very next game, that is, when Manuel Neuer got his pocket pinched on the edge of the South Korean penalty area, and Hyeung Min Son chased a long punt the length of the pitch to clinch a 2-0 win. You had to write them off then, no choice in the matter. Presumably somewhere in Germany another commentator had just said that Neuer was inevitably going to grab the precious equaliser, and his Fate-tempting mojo simply overpowered everyone else's.

Has there ever been, though, a starker example of the perils of hubris, of Fate being carelessly and repeatedly jabbed into retaliatory action, than the campaign waged by Ally McLeod's Scotland side at the 1978 World Cup? From the moment they qualified, Scotland's fans and, it has to be said, their charismatic manager eschewed the 'taking one game at a time' play-it-safe approach, and went straight for the 'we're going to win it!' message that absolutely no one with any sense ever spouts.

Because, the thinking went, 'Why not Scotland? Eh?'

After all, hadn't Scotland been the only undefeated team in the 1974 tournament, going out on goal difference after draws with Brazil and Yugoslavia. The winners, West Germany, had lost to the East Germans in their group match, whereupon they were written off. (Never do that, by the way.)

Had they not qualified ahead of the European champions, the Panenka-penalty sporting Czechoslovakia? Did that not make them the top team in Europe (because that's how that sort of thing always works)?

And there were only sixteen teams in the tournament, so they were already through to the last sixteen.

For the second World Cup in a row Scotland had qualified and England had not, which meant that the national press and the television pundits really got the wind in their sails, puffing them up, goading them to further bragging, seemingly taking the team to their hearts in a way that the Scotland supporters simultaneously felt was absolutely right and fair and yet also deeply irritating. It was the Andy Murray Paradox writ large: when he's winning Wimbledon he's British, when his hip is knackered he's a Scot.

Thousands of ginger be-wigged kilt wearers were making the trip to South America to see history made. Some were trying to charter a submarine.

Top of the Pops was again plastered in tartan as comedian Andy Cameron brought *Ally's Tartan Army* into the charts, cheerfully bellowing:

'We're on the march wi' Ally's Army

We're going to the Argentine

An' we'll really shake 'em up, when we win the World Cup

'Cos Scotland are the greatest football team'

Of course, this sort of thing has been sung by football fans for ever – when Oldham do it we substitute the phrase 'the World Cup' with the Autoglass Windshield Trophy, or similar –

but Ally's Tartan Army tapped into and fuelled a real belief that this braggadocio was merely a statement of fact.

Fate might have remained indifferent, but then Scotland had an open-top bus parade before they even set off, ending up in an underwhelmingly under-populated Hampden Park – tickets were 50p – on a motorcade of sponsored Vauxhalls. And once the actual football began, she was merciless.

Joe Jordan put McLeod's boys ahead against Peru, but then Teofilo Cubillas masterminded a 3-1 victory for the South Americans that was a shock really only to the Scots, for whom Don Masson duffed a penalty.

They then barely scraped a draw against no-hopers Iran, thanks to an Eskandarian own goal, and had to send Willie Johnston home in disgrace following a failed drugs test. I vividly recall the yellow colouring of whatever tablets he took leaking all over somebody's sweaty palm at an embarrassing press conference.

I vividly recall, also, the shot of a despairing Ally McLeod sitting on the bench with his head in his hands.

All of which left them facing Holland (later trading as the Netherlands), last time's runners up, needing to win by three clear goals to go forwards. The Dutch were without the great Cruyff, who had allegedly stayed away in a protest (surprisingly grown-up for a footballer) against the Argentinian ruling junta, though it later turned out that he'd been rattled by a kidnap attempt on his family in Barcelona the year before and didn't want to leave them.

Fate now decided to give Scotland a tantalising glimpse of what might have been if they hadn't ticked her off, and if McLeod hadn't left Graeme Souness on the bench for the first two games.

Robbie 'Rent-a-brick' Rensenbrinck put the Dutch ahead with a penalty. Then Kenny Dalglish equalised just before half time, and just after it Archie Gemmill also scored a penalty. With just over twenty minutes left, Gemmill then danced into the opposition penalty area, leaving defenders in his wake, and scored a beautiful, beautiful goal.

'Scotland are in Dreamland!' cried David Coleman, and just one more goal would have made everything all right, but very soon after that Johnny Rep made it 3-2, and the moment had passed.

In a cruel and unusually amusing move, the Dutch later presented Ally McLeod with a souvenir egg timer, to represent the three minutes that Scotland actually spent in Dreamland.

In the end, the 1978 World Cup in Argentina was memorable for several things. The ticker-tape confetti showering down from the stands, which made it look like the whole tournament was taking place in a snow-globe, and which led to much copycat behaviour the following season, and left a 1978-79 shaped gap in many a programme collection.

Then there was the transparent corruption that allowed Argentina to reach the final. Needing to win by four, they stuck six goals past Peru's Argentine-born keeper, a feat in no way helped by the Argentine junta suddenly releasing a grain subsidy that would make life significantly more comfortable for many in Peru.

And of course the final itself, with the controversy over van der Kerkhov's arm cast, which nobody else had complained about in all his previous games. Rent-a-brick hitting the post with a chance which would have won not only the Cup for his country but also the Golden Boot for himself. But then in extra time, Mario Kempes clinching both.

However colourful and exciting it was – and it was – the 1978 World Cup will always be above all a cautionary tale for football fans everywhere. Don't tempt Fate – she'll kick you in the sporran.

On
Wilderness Years

The 1970s were a horribly difficult time to be an English football supporter. Let's face it, the English have always had a bit of a superiority complex when it comes to football. After all, we invented the game, didn't we, and codified it. England barely lost a game until the 1950s, when those freakish Hungarians smashed us home and away.

When foreigners started up their own tournaments the English would typically not even deign to dignify these with our presence. We disdained the first few World Cups, only joining in when FIFA practically begged us to take part in 1950 to legitimise the whole shambolic pantomime for them. And we obliged by losing to the United States, thus bringing them headlines around the world.

Similarly, when the European Cup started up, our champions didn't enter at first, owing to the English football administrators' distrust of anything cooked up by Johnny Foreigner.

Our sense of entitlement was only bolstered by the 1966 World Cup triumph, of course, and buttressed by Manchester

United's European Cup win in 1968, and by the sense that England were the only team that could match the mighty Brazilians in 1970 (even though we lost to the West Germans, but that was because of the heat and Gordon Banks's gippy tummy).

From this point, the high point of our self-regard, the next decade felt like one long reality check, one long tumble down to earth, one prolonged sequence of kicks in the teeth.

There was the 1972 European Nations Cup, in which England succumbed at home to the West Germans, unable to handle the brilliance of Gunther Netzer. The West Germans went on to win that one, beating the USSR in the final.

Then there was the 1974 World Cup, for which England failed to qualify. It all came down to a must-win game at Wembley against Poland, and the nation was anxious but confident, given that Ramsey's men had beaten Austria 7-0 just four weeks earlier. Brian Clough's pre-match punditry famously included describing Jan Tomaszewski, the Poles' keeper, as a 'clown'. England had many chances, but Tomaszewski was able to keep them out with the help of his over-sized shoes and a revolving bow-tie, and it was Poland who took the lead through Domarski. Allan Clarke equalised for the spot, but England couldn't find a winner, having a last-gasp effort by late sub Kevin Hector cleared off the line. Poland went to the World Cup, where they finished third (behind West Germany, who won again).

As if it wasn't bad enough sitting on the sidelines England fans had to endure the bitter pill of watching Scotland strut their stuff on the big stage, and what's more return home unbeaten. And if you wanted any more proof that Brian Clough knew what he was talking about, you should know that Jan

Tomaszewski was elected to the Polish parliament in 2001 as an MP representing the conservative Law and Justice part, thereby joining a whole bunch of clowns.

Sir Alf Ramsey paid the price for failure to qualify once it became clear that he was not going to resign of his own accord, and, after a sunny interregnum under Joe Mercer, the England job passed to Don Revie, manager of the League champions, Leeds United. Revie and his team were respected but not especially popular, it has to be said, and he never really won over the England fans or the press.

There were, however, some highlights to enjoy during Revie's dour reign, notably a victory over the West Germans in a friendly at Wembley masterminded by debutant Alan Hudson. But Revie's mistrust of so-called flair players meant that this was a false dawn, as Hudson won only one more cap. Gerry Francis looked a world-beater in a 5-1 win over Scotland at Wembley, but sadly injuries curtailed a promising international career for the new captain.

England missed out on the 1976 European Championships to Czechoslovakia, who went on to win the whole thing, ultimately beating the West Germans thanks to Panenka's audacious penalty shoot-out winner.

After England lost a World Cup qualifier away to Italy Revie began to feel the heat. He felt that he had lost the support of the FA, and the papers were getting on his back. While his team were in South America playing friendly draws against Brazil and Argentina he was said to be in Finland diligently scouting our next qualifying opponents. In fact, however, he was in the United Arab Emirates negotiating himself a coaching contract there, and he resigned once this story broke.

Ron Greenwood was the new man in charge, a genial fellow

who had been a successful manager of West Ham where he had been instrumental in the careers of Bobby Moore, Geoff Hurst and Martin Peters, among others. He had stepped upstairs at Upton Park to a general manager's role, and so he seemed to be coming out of a sort of semi-retirement to take over England. Nonetheless he was well-liked and well-respected, and did his best with the mess Revie had left behind.

England's two best players, Kevin Keegan and Trevor Brooking, combined to cancel out our earlier defeat to Italy in the rematch at Wembley, but our overly-pragmatic failure to put group minnows Finland and Luxembourg to the sword ended up costing us, and we finished behind the Italians on goal difference and missed out again.

Which meant that once again we were forced to grit our teeth and pretend to support Scotland as they went off to the World Cup in Argentina.

It's tempting to just shrug and put these wilderness years down to the fact that English football wasn't much cop, but it was actually a kind of golden age for English club football.

Liverpool won the European Cup in 1977 and 1978. Then Brian Clough's Nottingham Forest won it in 1979 and 1980. On into the 1980s Liverpool won it again in 1981 and Aston Villa lifted it in 1982. Post-Revie Leeds under Jimmy Armfield got to the final in 1975 (where they lost to some Germans, which was a bit of a theme of the period).

Liverpool, Tottenham and Ipswich Town enjoyed success in the UEFA Cup, while in the European Cup Winners Cup West Ham reached the final in 1976, as did Arsenal in 1980.

In addition, England could call on the European Footballer of the Year of 1978 and 1979 in Kevin Keegan (of SV Hamburg) and the first million-pound footballer in Trevor Francis.

And there was a feeling that England not only had the best goalkeeper in the world in Ray Clemence (or Peter Shilton), but also the second-best in Peter Shilton (or Ray Clemence) and the third as well (Joe Corrigan).

Surely this should all have translated into a bit of success – a qualification or two, at least – for the England team? Ron Greenwood even appeared to acknowledge this thought by stuffing his first selections with Liverpool players, including a surprise comeback for 1966 veteran Ian Callaghan and of course the presence of the recently-departed red legend Keegan, in an attempt to recreate this club-level progress.

It's a bit of a mystery that we didn't do better, even taking into account Sir Alf passing his sell-by date and Revie's off-putting pragmatism. What is certain, though, is that by the time the 1980s got under way England were more than ready to return to the top table.

On
Ron's 22

'This time, more than any other time, we'll get it right.'

These were the words sung on *Top of the Pops*, with varying degrees of enthusiasm, by England's squad for the 1982 World Cup. Kevin Keegan was front and centre, flush from the Euro-pop success of his solo single *Head over Heels in Love*, released while he was at SV Hamburg and European Footballer of the Year to boot – not that you could see his boots in those massive flared trousers he was wearing.

If only Keegan had been fit to appear front and centre during the actual matches, 1982 might have been a different story.

England qualified for the World Cup in Spain, the first time they'd managed this feat for twenty years. They'd made it as hosts in 1966, of course, and as holders in 1970, but then had vacated the world stage for a dozen years. It helped that FIFA had tinkered with the format, meaning there were 24 places up for grabs rather than 16. Even so England needed all the help they could get, losing three matches in qualifying. They lost their away games to Romania, to Switzerland – after which the players had to talk Ron Greenwood out of retiring on the plane home – and to Norway, a humiliation that inspired one of the greatest pieces of commentary ever from Norwegian commentator Bjorn Lillelien.

He began by shouting: 'We are best in the world! We have beaten England!' – which strongly suggested he hadn't been paying attention throughout the previous decade. He then went on to taunt a hilarious roll call of English icons:

'Lord Nelson! Lord Beaverbrook! Sir Winston Churchill! Clement Attlee! Henry Cooper! Lady Diana! We have beaten them all! Maggie Thatcher, can you hear me?! Maggie Thatcher – your boys took a hell of a beating! Your boys took a hell of a beating!'

Lord Beaverbrook is outstanding work there, almost as comical as the idea that Thatcher would have given a damn about an England result of any kind. Theresa May demonstrated that she is cut from exactly the same cloth during the 2018 tournament when she was presented with a shirt by the Belgian Prime Minister on the eve of our group stage clash, and clearly it hadn't occurred to her to reciprocate, or to even be aware that our two countries were engaged in anything other than the grim task of trying to extricate the UK from Europe whilst remaining inextricably attached to Europe.

So England limped to their first World Cup in twelve years in second place behind Hungary, and hoped to do better than at Euro 1980, where they had gone out after a draw with Belgium and a defeat to Italy, winning only a dead rubber against Spain.

Greenwood had come under fire for using 19 players in those three matches, and for alternating goalkeepers Ray Clemence and Peter Shilton, as though he couldn't make up his mind and wanted to treat everyone as equals.

As if to reinforce this impression, the squad numbering for 1982 was alphabetical, apart from the keepers and captain Keegan,, who nabbed the number 7, leading to some good quiz question possibilities. Who was number nine? Not Paul Mariner or Trevor Francis or Peter Withe – it was Glenn Hoddle. Who was England's number 3? Not Kenny Sansom, but Trevor Brooking.

The number 3 and the number 7, arguably Greenwood's two key players, the ones that made the team tick, were both carrying injuries as the tournament approached, and England were obliged to begin with Ipswich Town's Mick Mills as stand-in captain. We did have rising star Bryan Robson to get enthusiastic about, though, and he scored after twenty-seven seconds of the opening group game against France as England started the tournament like a train.

They won all three group games, beating France 3-1 and Czechoslovakia 2-0, before a narrow 1-0 win over minnows Kuwait started to breed the sneaking suspicion that the train was running out of steam, and shortly thereafter track.

The format put teams in a second round three-team round robin, and we ended up with West Germany, naturally, and the hosts Spain. After a goalless draw with the Germans we needed to beat Spain by two to make the semi-finals. Midway through the second half Greenwood finally threw on the half-fit Keegan and Brooking for their first appearances of the tournament. Keegan had a great chance to break the deadlock with an unmarked header from just a few yards out, but he somehow glanced it wide of the post.

In their not altogether pleasant red, white and blue pullovers they had sung: 'We're gonna find a way, find a way to get away, this time…' What did that mean? As it turned out, they'd certainly found a way to get away from being in the tournament any more, despite not losing a game and only conceding one goal. This time, less than any other time, nobody talked Ron Greenwood out of retiring, and it was Ipswich Town's Bobby Robson who took on the job.

Without England, the 1982 tournament certainly generated some memorable moments. Gerry Armstrong's surprise winner for ten-man Northern Ireland against Spain, for one, and David Narey's blistering opener for Scotland against Brazil (not a winner, unfortunately).

As a neutral, it was easy to get excited about watching Brazil, and also France. Brazil had dumped the cautious pragmatism of their 1970s sides and were finally beginning to play thrilling sunlit football like their predecessors. Their sumptuously talented midfield of Falcao, Cerezo, Eder and Zico was topped off by their chain-smoking captain Socrates, and their willingness to play almost a 2-7-1 formation inevitably led to goals at both ends.

They ran up against an Italy side who were being slaughtered at home for a miserably uninspiring group stage performance which had brought them three draws. Italy's only striking option was Paolo Rossi, who was returning without much in the way of match practice from a two-year ban for his involvement in a notorious betting scandal, and he was described as wandering around like a ghost in the first stage. Come the game with Brazil, however, Rossi returned back to life, and grabbed a hat-trick as Italy won the game of the tournament 3-2.

The other neutrals' favourites, Michel Platini's France, met West Germany in the semi-final. It was a highly dramatic game, overshadowed by the moment when Patrick Battiston ran through one-on-one with the German keeper Harald

Schumacher and was flattened. First Schumacher smashed into the Frenchman's hip, before bashing out two teeth, breaking three ribs and knocking him out cold. It wasn't a red card, or even a free kick. He should have been sent to jail. But no, he was still around to save two penalties in the shootout, as West Germany made it to the final (again).

Italy hit their stride for the final, winning 3-1 thanks to Paolo Rossi's Golden Boot clinching opener, Marco Tardelli – whose open-mouthed out-of-control celebration run is the image of the whole tournament – and Alessandro Altobelli. Perhaps it's better not to start a tournament well after all.

So at least the Germans didn't win it, which is something. And even though 1982 felt like a failure, four years later FIFA published rankings for all previous World Cups which placed England sixth, just behind that brilliant Brazil team.

And at least we'd got back into the habit of qualifying for things. Hadn't we…?

On
Mascots

I don't know what it is about mascots, but I don't like them. They don't seem to me to belong in football, they seem to belong to another sport, probably an American one.

I'm talking about the blokes in giant foam-and-fur animal costumes who walk around the touchline waving at kids, although it's never quite clear whether they can actually see out, and if so where from. Rather that, though, than the small children who come out holding the players' hands for the line-up-and-shake-hands at the beginning, which I also dislike. Especially the bit where one of them gets to pick the match ball up off a plinth as they walk out, as though it was some kind of treasure rather than something that can be replaced in the first minute of the game when the visiting centre half boots it over the low stand and into the car park. Unless of course it's a kid like the McDonalds competition winner at the World Cup in 2002 who was taller and considerably beefier than the player rather nervously holding his hand.

A friend of mine used to do mascot work – not at football,

I hasten to add, but in shopping precincts. He would arrive in a van with a handful of similarly under-employed actors and the costumes would be handed out. He usually got Postman Pat, which was apparently a nightmare because you couldn't see anything looking downwards on account of Pat's enormous bulbous nose, and once children worked this out they would dodge under there and kick his shins.

Most clubs seem to regard them as indispensable these days, and in fairness I suppose you can sometimes get a grown-up laugh out of them. The famous time Wolfie the Wolves mascot tried to beat up Bristol City's Three Little Pigs for instance. Or when Sam Allardyce raged at the Watford mascot Harry the Hornet for taking the piss out of a Wilfried Zaha dive. Or the apocryphal story about Cyril the Swan of Swansea decapitating Millwall's Zampa the Lion and drop-kicking his head into the stands. Or the inexplicable grotesquerie of the Partick Thistle mascot Kingsley, which looks like the sun-baby off of *Teletubbies* has lost it and is about to go on a murderous rampage.

When my kids were small they always looked out for Oldham's mascot, Chaddy the Owl, who had by the way a really great record in the annual mascot race because the costume didn't include over-sized costume feet so he could just run in trainers. Chaddy is named after the 'Chaddy End' – the Chadderton Road end – of Boundary Park. One time the costume was replaced, and the club commissioned a local seamstress to do the job, which was a cheap and very poor idea. Children screamed when they saw it, and their parents told them to be good or else 'Chaddy will get you'. Like a cuddly Freddie Krueger.

Chaddy did make me laugh one time, when he abandoned the mascot's cheerful disposition and became just like the rest of us fans, embittered and perpetually disappointed. Oldham had just let in a fifth goal at home to Wrexham, and he fell to his knees and began banging his big cuddly owl head on the advertising hoardings.

Occasionally the mascot will have a mate-for-the-day, another character there to promote something on a one-off basis. West Brom's, for instance, was recently joined by a man dressed as a combi boiler on legs thanks to a new sponsorship deal. And once, at Walsall, I caught sight of a bloke dressed in a most peculiar way. His costume was pink, and had wiry black protusions all over it. It was vaguely saddle-shaped, I supposed, and Walsall were the Saddlers, so I thought maybe that was the explanation. When he came round our side of the pitch, though, you could see that he was intended to promote prostate cancer awareness, and was in fact a sort of giant upside-down scrotum.

'How was your day, dear?'

'I was a giant upside-down scrotum, how do you think it was?'

On
Sir Bobby Robson

Bobby Robson was old school. This is his almost Ron Manager-esque quote about the very idea of a football club:

> 'What is a club in any case? Not the buildings or the directors or the people who are paid to represent it. It's not the television contracts, get-out clauses, marketing departments or executive boxes. It's the noise, the passion, the feeling of belonging, the pride in your city. It's a small boy clambering up the stadium steps for the very first time, gripping his father's hand, gawping at that hallowed stretch of turf beneath him, and without being able to do a thing about it, falling in love.'

His enthusiasm was infectious, and his avuncular charm irresistible, even if he did sometimes forget a player's name or two. 'Good morning, Bobby,' he once apparently said to Bryan Robson, who replied:

'No Gaffer, you're Bobby, I'm Bryan'.

How could you have anything but affection for a manager who could do that?

Bobby Robson became a national treasure, such a beloved figure in English football – in world football even – that it's easy to forget how vilified he was during his time as England manager. He was the first to come under that intense scrutiny and pressure from the tabloid press that has become the norm, and arguably provided the first taste of blood that stirred the feeding frenzy that has gone on ever since.

Robson's first act on taking over from Ron Greenwood in 1982 was to draw a line under the international career of tabloid favourite Kevin Keegan. There were grumblings about this, but a sequence of decent results in Euro 84 qualification, including a 9-0 thrashing of Luxembourg – there were easy games in those days, unlike today, apparently – kept the press onside. Until, that is, a defeat to Denmark ended England's hopes, and *The Sun* produced its first '*Robson Out!*' badges.

Robson offered his resignation, but Bert Millichip, the chairman of the FA, refused to accept it, perhaps alarmed at the likelihood that he would be obliged to hire Brian Clough. So instead of going to France, where Michel Platini would take the home nation to glory with 9 goals in 5 matches, Robson took his England team to Brazil, where he silenced his critics, for a while at least, with a memorable 2-0 win in the Maracana, illuminated by a brilliant goal from John Barnes.

That Denmark defeat turned out to be Robson's only defeat in 28 qualifying games in charge, and he took a strong-looking squad to Mexico for the 1986 World Cup. To begin with, the knives were being sharpened again as England lost their opener to Portugal, and then drew 0-0 with Morocco.

Then Robson got lucky. He'd started the tournament with Mark Hateley up front, Gary Lineker playing off him, and a midfield axis of Bryan Robson and Ray Wilkins.

Bryan Robson was still recovering from a dislocated shoulder, all strapped up with gaffer tape, which popped out again during the Morocco game. England's prospects were further diminished when Wilkins got himself sent off for chucking a ball at the referee. Or *to* the referee, as Wilkins himself would doubtless have said.

So Bobby Robson was forced to change things around, creating a totally revamped midfield. In came Peter Reid, Steve Hodge and Trevor Steven to join Glenn Hoddle, and the clever Peter Beardsley came in for Hateley to link the midfield to Lineker. It seemed to click right away. Hoddle revelled in the greater responsibility, and Beardsley made himself a fixture in the side for years to come with his smart link-up play.

England beat Poland 3-0 to go through, then Paraguay by the same score in the last 16, with Lineker notching five of the goals.

If Bryan Robson hadn't fallen apart, and if Ray Wilkins hadn't flipped, completely out of character, would England have crashed out early? Would Bobby Robson have made way, perhaps for Brian Clough?

As it was, England reached the quarter-final, where they put up a decent fight against eventual winners Argentina, beaten by the Hand of God thing and then that other thing that the legitimate body parts of God did later. Gary Lineker carted home the Golden Boot, which was nice, and the campaign was accounted a success.

England then qualified easily for Euro 88 but the tournament itself was disastrous. Gary Lineker, who had been in fine goal-scoring form, was unwell and below par, and England lost all three group games, to Ireland, the Netherlands and Russia.

The Sun headline screamed: 'In The Name of God, Go!' which seemed a bit much. After all, what did Maradona have to do with it? Robson offered his resignation once again, and once again Bert Millichip refused it, as Brian Clough was still a looming presence. That headline was amended to: 'In The Name of Allah, Go!', after a limp draw with Saudi Arabia – imagine the reaction you'd get to that one now – and the press were nipping at Robson's heels all the way through qualification for Italia 90.

In the end they pressured Millichip into saying that Robson needed to win the World Cup or he'd be out. Robson, reasonably enough, took the precaution of accepting a job at PSV Eindhoven. Now the press started tearing strips off him for being disloyal and unpatriotic for lining up a job abroad.

Effectively, the tabloids had driven Robson out, by hookwinking the FA into believing that they represented a tide of popular opinion. The tabloids purported to be speaking for football fans everywhere, but of course they were not. And along the way they helped to establish that unthinking sense of entitlement that has hamstrung every England team since – that feeling that nothing less than winning tournaments and beating everyone that stands in our way will do.

In the event, Robson led England to the semi-finals of Italia 90, the second-best result in the nation's history, and more than good enough to have guaranteed him at least another four years at the helm. Did the tabloids feel foolish, guilty at all, for having deprived the national team of the services of its second-most successful manager? Did they learn their lesson, and give his successors an easier ride?

Of course not. They had tasted blood, and the England manager was fair game. The post was even dubbed 'The Impossible Job' by those who had made it so. Over the next decade and a half Robson went on to demonstrate what the FA and the tabloid press had thrown away. He went on to win two league titles with PSV Eindhoven, two more with Porto, and a Cup and a Cup-Winners' Cup with Barcelona. He took Newcastle United into the Champions League twice.

He was a mentor to Jose Mourinho and Andre Villas-Boas, and was described as one of the greatest coaches ever by one of the great players, original Ronaldo. And he was even, tantalisingly, offered the chance to take the job on again part-time, impossible as it was, when Kevin Keegan stepped down in 2001, but Newcastle wouldn't let him. Oh well.

On
The English Disease

In the 1970s and 1980s hooliganism was such a feature of the football landscape, both at home and when English clubs and the national team travelled abroad, that it became known as 'The English Disease'.

Manchester United fans were particularly notorious in the mid-1970s. I was at the game in 1974 when Denis Law back-heeled his former club into what was then called the Second Division and then burst into tears, wiping his nose on his light blue Manchester City sleeve. My Granddad and I were right behind that goal, courtesy of a couple of season tickets that a friend of his had given up using through disillusionment, and as soon as Law's deftly treacherous dagger hit the back of the net he grabbed me by the wrist and started hauling me towards the exit. I wanted to see the final minute or two play out, but my Granddad knew what was about to happen. Sure enough, when we got back to his house for tea there were pictures on the news of the pitch invasion by dozens of yobs in parkas and flares, hair mulleted like Noddy Holder, scarves tied to wrists in the fashion of the day – and looking uncannily, from my hindsighted perspective, like the crowd that invade the pitch at the end of *Escape to Victory*, simultaneously thirty years earlier and seven years later.

This event neatly encapsulates my experience of football hooliganism, in that I was aware of it, certainly, knew that it happened, but never actually saw it myself. It always seemed to me that those who wanted to get involved in hooliganism got together with other like-minded individuals from other 'firms', and got on with whatever they wanted to get up to wherever they decided they would do that, and if you didn't want any part of it you would just manage to avoid it without too much effort.

I was once on a radio show and one of the other guests was Cass Pennant, the now reconstructed former hooligan and author. When I suggested that I had never personally been involved in or ever seen any violence he earnestly and somewhat sorrowfully gave me chapter and verse of violent incidents that had happened at Oldham matches down the years, many of which I had attended. All I could say was I hadn't seen it.

One time, just one, I was shoved around a bit by a bully at an away game in Derby. I know you're supposed to stand up to bullies, but since this one was sitting on a police horse I decided to let it go.

I was certainly aware of the knock-on effects of hooliganism. Everyone was. That Manchester United side, the one that was relegated to the Second Division, caused so much mayhem in towns and grounds up and down the land that clubs began to introduce segregation and fencing inside their grounds. Indeed, Old Trafford was the first to bring this in and everyone followed suit.

I recall going to Rotherham United's Millmoor from time

to time as a kid with a mate and his dad, and we used to like to watch the first half from one end and then go round behind the other goal for the second half, but the fear of hooliganism, even though we never saw any, put paid to that little treat.

In the 1970s and 1980s there was no shortage of news items about the English disease. Leeds United were banned from Europe after their fans rioted in Paris when their team were beaten by Bayern Munich in the European Cup final. Dozens were injured during a notorious riot at Millwall during an FA Cup quarter-final with Ipswich Town. England fans were tear-gassed in Turin – England players, too, inadvertently – during the 1980 Euro game with Belgium.

It was around then that Margaret Thatcher began to want to stick her oar in. She'd given Ron Greenwood's men a Downing Street send-off – she was particularly chummy with Emlyn Hughes, I seem to remember – and felt personally affronted by the disgraceful scenes. The Prime Minister wasn't averse to making political capital out of sport. She desperately wanted to join her buddy Ronald Reagan's boycott of the 1980 Olympics in Moscow over the invasion of Afghanistan – remember when the American president used to complain about things the Russians did? – and she also wanted to withdraw from the 1982 World Cup because of the tension created by the Falklands War. Both times, however, she was thwarted by the governing bodies' reluctance to allow her to sideline them and thus negate their very raison d'être.

There was an undeniably nasty political dimension to football hooliganism. Racist and right wing groups like the National Front were attaching themselves to hooligan groups, cashing in on the abuse of the increasing numbers of black players appearing for British teams.

This association was difficult to deal with for decent football fans, and for a time even admitting to liking football at all caused people to look at you suspiciously. You watch it on the television, yeah, but you don't actually go to games, do you?

In 1985 football hooliganism was beginning to seem an intractable problem. A riot involving the fans of Millwall and Luton Town was all over the news, with pictures of torn-up seats raining down onto the pitch. Thatcher's government responded by setting up a 'war cabinet' to deal with the issue.

The Minister for Sport, Colin Moynihan, a diminutive former boat race cox who was brilliantly dubbed by *Spitting Image* 'Colin Miniman, the miniature for Sport' (different times), was tasked with introducing an identity card system for football fans. Any fool could see that wasn't going to work, and would result in the end of casual football watching at a stroke. It was clear, too, that the only purpose in having them was so that they could be withdrawn.

This was Thatcher's approach, though, to things she had no particular empathy with – most humans fell into that category – she would try to wipe them out. It had worked with the miners and the Argentinians, and those triumphs had cemented her authority and earned her the soubriquet 'The Iron Lady'. Football was a little different as it turned out, and more resistant to destruction, although not at all averse to giving the appearance of trying to destroy itself.

In 1985 the Chelsea chairman and Thatcher suck-up Ken Bates erected a twelve foot high barbed electric fence around the pitch. There had been a pitch invasion at Stamford Bridge a month earlier and Bates decided he would take the lead in the fight against hooliganism, milking all the publicity he could from his hard-line stance. The fence was due to be switched on – I'm presuming Bates had lined up Su Pollard for this, or perhaps Keith Harris and Orville – at a home fixture with Spurs, which, given the club's traditionally Jewish fan base, could be said to bring with it the worst possible associations for such a measure, but the GLC threatened legal action and it remained merely an offensively massive barbed wire fence.

Thatcher's government wrestled incompetently with the problem of football hooliganism for the next few years. Perhaps its finest scheme came to light a couple of years ago when some documents were released under what's known as 'the 30 years rule'.

It was Bernard Ingham, Thatcher's press secretary, who suggested a campaign called 'Goalies Against Hoolies' – not as it sounds an attempt to enlist the assistance of Peter Shilton and co to stamp out the plague of Irish dancing which, unchecked, ultimately resulted in *Riverdance*. The idea was that the nation's shot-stoppers were 'often first in line of hooligan fire', and that they could, well, what…? Reason with the yobbos? Persuade them to calm down? Talk them out of invading the playing area? Gary Bailey was singled out particularly because he was 'an articulate graduate', and we all know how well respected they are in the world of football.

This top level comic boobery was thrown into sharp relief by the events of May 1985, surely the darkest month in the long history of football. First there was the terrible fire at Bradford City, in which 56 people lost their lives. Not a hooligan incident, of course, but a ghastly tragedy which showed football's cavalier attitude to fans' safety, a horror that could not have occurred if all safety standards had been observed.

Then there was Heysel, and that definitely was a hooligan thing. At the European Cup final in a crumbling anachronism of a stadium in Brussels Liverpool fans broke through a police cordon and charged a section of the ground occupied by Juventus fans. The Italian supporters tried to escape, and a wall collapsed. 39 were crushed to death, and English football was disgraced.

English clubs were banned from European competitions - not just Liverpool, all of them – because after all this was an English Disease, and it demanded a radical cure. And those of us not remotely infected by it were nonetheless obliged to take the medicine.

On
The Hand of God

Even now, it makes me mad whenever I think about it. I can't even bring myself to write his name.

He runs at the heart of the packed England defence, no way through, knocks it out right. The ball pops up, and Steve Hodge gets under it and hacks it back high towards the penalty spot. Peter Shilton comes out to punch it clear, but he has continued his run and jumps to meet the England keeper. He realises he's not going to get there first to head it in, he's simply too squat, so he shoves a stubby little fist up above his head and punches it into the goal.

That's just the start, though, the start of the cheating. Next comes the selling it. He runs over to the advertising hoardings as though he's scored a perfectly good goal, a fair goal, he celebrates with the crowd, he celebrates with his team mates, utterly utterly brazen, like any shameless con man has to be.

It's no consolation that the Tunisian referee, Ali Bin Nassar, never took charge of another big game after failing to spot this chicanery – and after all Barry Davies didn't spot it first time through: he thought the England players were claiming offside until he saw the replay, the *blatantly obvious* replay. Before we let the referee off with mere incompetence, however, let us consider that the Bulgarian linesman maintained that he did see it but had been told not to question any decisions since he and the referee had no common language in which to communicate. He claimed the incident ruined his life. For his part, Bin Nassar later stated that his eyesight had been affected by a haemorrhoid treatment.

Even more gallingly, the cheat went on then to score another goal just a few minutes later, this one legitimate, which is acclaimed (not by me) as one of the best goals ever scored at a World Cup. Barry Davies's commentary brings the sun-bleached pictures vividly back to mind: 'You have to say that's magnificent!'

Well, not me. I have to say that's disgusting. The outright cheating devalues everything for me. There's no way he scores that second goal except in the aftermath of the first. He zigzags past England players whose wits are scrambled by the sheer mind-boggling unfairness of the punched-in goal. You say they are professionals, they have to get it back together, and they did, to get a goal back and nearly equalise through the trickery of John Barnes and the poaching of Gary Lineker, but how could you not be burning up inside after seeing that? Terry Fenwick admits that he would have brought the little swine down, except he had just been booked for protesting about the handball so he had to hold back.

Afterwards, when Argentina were through to the semi-final and England were out, the evidence was undeniable… or was it? With breathtaking arrogance he refused to apologise, refused even to acknowledge that he had done anything untoward. Apparently it was the Hand of God what done it.

In subsequent years, presumably realising that he was absolutely bang to rights as far as the court of international opinion was concerned, he admitted what he had done, but he managed to do this without once expressing a moment's contrition for besmirching the beautiful game with his loathsome antics. In 2005, for example, he said this: 'The truth is that I don't for a second regret scoring that goal with my hand'.

He was undeniably a tremendously skilful player, and guided his nation to the trophy in Mexico. When it comes to assessing where he belongs in football's pantheon, however, that success is built on a lie (thought admittedly it was a little bit amusing that they beat Germany in the final).

Let's look at his achievements from other World Cups.

In 1982 he was sent off for kicking a defender in the groin. All right, we've all wanted to do that, but something holds us back.

In 1990 he presumed that he was so beloved after leading Napoli to a *scudetto* that the locals would support him against their own national team. That's vanity for you, right there, up at a Cristiano Ronaldo level.

And in 1994 he did that god-awful demented roaring at the camera before failing a drugs test.

It's not exactly Pelé, is it? And he's done next-to-nothing to help those with erectile dysfunction, unlike the great Brazilian ambassador (see p.27).

Which reminds me: in his paid (£7,250 a game) capacity as a FIFA ambassador at the 2018 World Cup he covered himself with further glory by giving a stubby little two-middle-fingered salute to the Nigerian fans as Argentina scraped by them. And he was wearing two massive watches, one on each wrist – what was that about?

How, after failing a drugs test and being vilified worldwide as a despicable cheat, *how* can he then be feted as an ambassador by any but the most corrupt and unhinged organisation on the planet… oh no, wait, answered my own question there.

In 2002 a friend of mine found himself staying in a Tokyo hotel room next to the butterball FIFA ambassador himself, as confirmed by the two burly minders in the corridor outside. He claims to have put a glass to the wall to try and hear if the Hand of God was in action.

So, the greatest player of all time? No. Greatest cheat of all time? Certainly, with Manuel Neuer, Sergio Ramos and Thierry Henry vying for a place on the podium.

I couldn't help feeling a little disappointed a few years ago when good old Gary Lineker did a chummy first-name-terms interview with the old hoodwinker, as though it was just a bit of fun, all forgotten now, and anyway it's only a game. I like Gary Lineker, and I think he is the absolute best at what he does nowadays, but on that occasion he made a bad mis-step.

Peter Shilton, on the other hand, refused to meet his nemesis, turning down the photo-opportunity to shake the Hand of God. That's more like it.

On
The Great Disconnect

As the 1980s wound to a close and the 1990s loomed, football was in a dark place. There was a definite disconnect between football and the general public. A feeling that while football was fine for the people it was for, there was something distasteful abut it that was preventing it from reaching out to new punters, that would surely in the years ahead keep it more and more confined to its own fenced-off arenas and increasingly remote from the mainstream of national culture.

English clubs were still banned in disgrace from Europe because of the Heysel Disaster. Thatcher was still trying to work out some sort of identity card system for football fans, which threatened to stigmatise them irredeemably.

The Hillsborough Disaster of April 1989, in which 96 people, men, women and children, lost their lives at an FA Cup semi-final, cast a long and gloomy shadow. It would be wrong to call this simply an example of football hooliganism, but the various outbreaks of the English Disease over the preceding couple of decades certainly contributed to the conditions that led to the tragedy. The perimeter fencing that gave the victims nowhere to go once the crush started were introduced to prevent pitch invasions, to keep fans in their cages, and fear of a hooligan incident outside the ground seems to have dictated the decision to allow in the extra fans all at once that caused the fatal surge.

After Hillsborough and also Bradford serious questions were being asked about whether football stadia were fit for purpose, and people were wondering whether football itself was worth the candle any more. England fans would go to Italia 90 in numbers, as usual, but they were greeted by police with batons and water cannons, shepherded like cattle from station to stadium and back, with any small expression of indignation at this treatment being greeted harshly. They had earned this, make no mistake, with the yobbish reputation of the England fans both at club and international level, where any visit to a foreign land felt like an invitation to smash the place up and ruck with like-minded representatives of the host territory.

If you were a casual sort of a supporter – even if you weren't – it was hard not to feel repelled by the pictures of English football supporters abroad, alienated by them. It was annoying that people's perception of you when you mentioned that you were a football supporter could be coloured by stories of these louts on the rampage. The idea of following England at the World Cup seemed like craziness. Why would you put yourself through it? The games were all going to be on the telly after all.

Unexpectedly, however, football's reputation was approaching a big turning point.

On the Field

With the benefit of 20/20 hindsight we can see turning points coming, not least on the field of play itself. At the top, for instance, Liverpool, the dominant force in English football, were on their way to another league title, their sixth of the decade. They would have won it in 1989 too, but for a barely-credible last minute goal by Arsenal's Michael Thomas that nicked it at the death on goals scored, with points and goal difference level.

Manchester United were reaching the end of their patience with manager Alex Ferguson, who had failed to end a title drought going back to 1967. His resculpted team were much closer to the relegation battle than the business end of the table, and the prevailing wisdom was that if the Reds had been knocked out of the FA Cup by Nottingham Forest he'd have been sacked. In the event a goal by youngster Mark Robins saved Fergie's neck, and he bought himself enough time to continue United's resurgence by winning the Cup.

Who would have thought that in the next twenty-eight years Liverpool would not win a single title, while Ferguson would win 13? Who'd have thought that England would reach two World Cup semi-finals without Liverpool being able to call themselves champions again?

As a fan of Oldham Athletic, I can safely say that the 1989-90 season and the one that followed it were the most enjoyable I have ever watched. Joe Royle put together a side from players rescued from the reserve squads of Manchester City, Everton and Leeds United that played some of the most exhilarating attacking football around, and for a time we became everybody's second favourite team.

Oldham played 65 games in 1989-90 thanks to two thrilling yet exhausting cup runs, and won nothing, but they were the team of the season by a mile. We'd not beaten a top-flight club for 66 years, but this term we beat Arsenal, the champions, 3-1. We beat Villa, the league leaders, 3-0. We beat Everton (who tried to kick us off the park by the way) and we beat Southampton, both after replays. We took Manchester United all the way in the FA Cup semi-final at Maine Road, only losing a replay after a fantastic 3-3 draw, while in the first leg of the League Cup semi-final we thrashed West Ham 6-0 in one of the most relentless displays of full-on attacking football you will ever see.

Brian Clough's Nottingham Forest beat us in the League Cup final by a single goal, but the legs had gone by then, as they had from the push for the play offs. Royle's rejects had already captivated the country, though. The following season, without the distraction of the cup runs, Oldham secured promotion to the First Division, winning the title with the last kick on their famous plastic pitch as Neil Redfearn clinched a 3-2 win over Sheffield Wednesday with a penalty kick that snatched the trophy from the hands of West Ham – who, embarrassingly, had already had their name engraved on it.

It's always a pleasure to remember Oldham's greatest ever team – Andy Rhodes or Jon Hallworth in goal, four of Denis Irwin, Earl Barrett, Paul Warhurst, Richard Jobson and Andy Barlow at the back, Nick Henry, Mike Milligan and/or Neil Redfearn in midfield, Neil Adams and Tricky Ricky Holden out wide, Andy Ritchie up front with six-goal Frankie Bunn or big Ian Marshall, not forgetting record scorer 'Oooh!' Roger Palmer. The group was assembled for less than a million quid, and I mention them here because they seem to me to represent something that changed at this point in football history or very shortly after – a seat-of-the-pants adventure that was possible and which has been rendered impossible to repeat by what followed.

What followed was Italia 90.

On
Italia 90

The 1990 World Cup in Italy is always referred to as Italia 90. It was the first to be known only by this kind of abbreviation, conferring a particularly affectionate aura on the memory of that tournament, which was a glorious coming-together of the essentials of football. No tournament before or since has quite pulled off what Italia 90 managed, although almost all of them have claimed to, or so it seems to me, including naturally the most recent one in Russia. Which was good, don't get me wrong. Italia 90, though, was so good it changed the course of football history, not altogether for the good, but certainly for good.

Think of Italia 90, think of *Nessun Dorma*, the soaring and emotional aria which the BBC chose as the theme for its coverage, which still sets the hairs up on the back of my neck.

Think of 'World in Motion', the coolest England World Cup song ever recorded, with its somehow-not-naff John Barnes rap about going round the back, and the message 'Express Yourself'.

Think of the best England kit ever, the white shirts with the dark collar, those rich blue shorts riding high up the thighs of men who weren't ashamed of their gleaming quads. Too high if we're talking about Stuart Pearce, but perhaps that explained the sheer intensity of his play.

Think of Gazza, think of Toto Schillaci, think of Roger Milla.

Think of games played in football-mad cities: Rome, Turin, Genoa, Milan, Florence, Naples, cities with history steeped in gladiatorial contests, cities with a seemingly endless supply of small horn-honking Fiats with blokes leaning out of the windows waving giant flags.

Statisticians will try to tell you that fewer goals per game were scored at Italia 90 than at the other tournaments, and that consequently it was somehow dull, but don't listen to them, don't let them reduce a memorable and visceral tournament to a mere breakdown of numbers. Italia 90 was the best. It was absorbing, thrilling, and ultimately – as football pretty much always is – heart-breaking, and it lingers in the memory like no other tournament since.

It didn't start particularly well, though, it has to be said. I have already mentioned how the FA finally gave in to the drip-drip-drip malevolent belittling of Bobby Robson in his years as England manager, and allowed themselves to be backed into a corner, declaring that if he didn't win the World Cup the manager would be sacked. In the face of this ultimatum Robson quite reasonably found another job, at PSV Eindhoven, whereupon he was mouth-frothingly vilified as a traitor by the self-same hacks who'd demanded his head. By the time the tournament drew near the FA had announced that his replacement would be Graham Taylor.

Taylor had just taken Aston Villa to the runners-up spot behind Liverpool. Check out Graham Taylor's career and he was runner up a lot of times. Got a lot of promotions, that's for sure, but always (bar the very first time with Lincoln City) in second place. He got Watford all the way (by repeatedly finishing second) to the top division (where he finished second) and to the Cup Final (where he also finished second). Finishing second is an admirable skill to have, unless you are the England manager and you have difficult qualification groups to negotiate where only the winner goes through.

England were in the last group to kick off, and the news surrounding the opener against the Republic of Ireland was all about the England fans being treated like animals, herded to and from the stadium in Cagliari by carabinieri and Italian military special forces, water cannons at the ready. England had been confined to Sardinia at the request of the British government, amid hysterical fears that a hooligan outbreak on the mainland of Italy might lead to a breakdown in diplomatic relations with the host nation.

The game itself wasn't great, not up to the standard we had already been treated to in, for example, the terrific opening game in which champions Argentina were toppled by nine-man Cameroon. England took an early lead through Gary Lineker, which they then sat on nervously until they conceded an inevitable equaliser to Kevin Sheedy late in the second half. The English press, unable to contain their glee at our apparent humiliation on and off the field of play, demanded that the FA 'Bring Them Home!'

A much better performance followed in the second game against the Netherlands of Ruud Gullit and Marco van Basten. Robson played three centre halves in Terry Butcher, Mark Wright and Des Walker in a move that was rumoured to be a result of player-power but which the manager later always claimed as a ploy of his own devising. Whatever, it freed Paul

Gascoigne to sparkle, dribbling past defenders here, nutmegging them there, twisting their blood as the old-timers used to say. It was only a 0-0 in the end – England had a Stuart Pearce free kick in the net which was disallowed for some reason – but nonetheless there was a feeling that a world star was born. On the flip side, Bryan Robson crocked himself again, as he had in 1986, and was on his way home, but again, as he had been in 1986, Bobby Robson was lucky. His captain's unfortunate departure opened the door for another young star to rise, Aston Villa's David Platt, soon to be promoted from impact sub to midfield linchpin.

It was beginning to seem like an irresistible festival of football and I wanted to go and have a look for myself. I didn't fancy being kettled in Sardinia, though, and so I took the opportunity to visit the mainland with some Scottish friends, which was great. The whole country had been taken over by football fever in a way that could never happen at home, such was the distance created by Heysel and Hillsborough, by fences and identity cards and baton charges. We went to see Scotland play Brazil in Turin, and saw the giant Fish from Marillion crammed into a tiny white Fiat taxi with his kneecaps actually pressed against the front windscreen. On a day trip to Florence we scored some tickets to USA v Austria, where more than half the crowd were listening to Italy play Czechoslovakia on transistor radios even as they watched the action in front of them. At the risk of contravening – pre-figuring, even – copyright, it was as if football had come home.

Back in England television audiences were captivated by the emergence of Gascoigne and Platt, who combined to create a heart-stopping last-minute-of-extra-time winner against Belgium in the first knockout round, a brilliant swivelling volley from a floated free kick that must rank as one of England's best ever moments.

Then the quarter-final against Cameroon, everyone's second favourite team, colourful, athletic, undeniably skilful, occasionally violent, took things to another level. Platt gave England the lead with a header, but then in the second half veteran super-sub Roger Milla carved us open and we were suddenly 2-1 down and facing a crushing disappointment. With just a few minutes to go, and then again in extra time, Gary Lineker broke through and was hacked to the ground, rising to slam home both penalties in emphatic fashion. And England were in the semi-final.

Twenty-six point two million people tuned in to watch England take on West Germany in that semi-final, an unheard of figure for any event that did not feature either Lady Diana in a wedding dress or Penelope Keith during an ITV strike which left only two channels available to an entertainment-starved population. Somewhere along the way football, the beautiful game, had managed to crawl out of its pit of shame and reconnect with the great British public in time for its finest hour since 1966. Tectonic plates were shifting, and although it was perhaps not apparent at that very moment, football was beginning to reinvent itself. The tabloid press which had called for the team to be brought home was left scrambling to catch up with the national mood. Bobby Robson was no longer a traitor, he was... why, he was a saint. The players were no longer a national disgrace, they were heroes one and all.

For the most important game of his life, Robson went with a front five of Platt, Gascoigne, Waddle, Beardsley and Lineker, and if there were not already many reasons to hold him in the highest affection then that would absolutely have done it for me.

And what a game it was. I have seen it many many times, for reasons I will go into shortly, and it was a truly high-class encounter. The Germans were the favourites, the best team around, muscular, clever and powerful, and England matched them every inch of the way. Robson's men went behind to a deflected free kick which looped up off Paul Parker and left Peter Shilton on his backside. Then they equalised with ten minutes to go when Gary Lineker nervelessly controlled a bouncing through ball from Parker on his thigh before tucking it into the corner.

Perhaps the most memorable moment of all came in extra time. Gazza slid into a tackle on Thomas Berthold, who rolled and rolled in feigned agony trying to get him booked. The referee, Jose Ramiz Wright of Brazil, bought it, and England's young star would miss the final if England got there. Tears cascaded down his cheeks, and his bottom lip jutted out, Gary Lineker mouthed to Robson to 'have a word with him', and every mother in the nation yearned to clasp the lad to her bosom.

We didn't know that penalties were our nemesis yet, but we didn't have a particularly good feeling about them. At three apiece Stuart Pearce, Bobby's banker, the dead-ball expert, slammed his kick against the German keeper's shins, and then Chris Waddle, shorn of mullet and certainty, punted his into orbit and the adventure was over.

The sea-change had happened, though, mystifyingly, and football would never be the same again. Thousands turned out to see Gazza return to Luton in a big pair of plastic false breasts that he somehow got away with (different times), and the nation had fallen in love with football all over again.

On
The Cultural Revolution

Insofar as the culture, if we can regard it as one whole thing, was interested in football, it was as the backdrop for a Theatre of Hate. *The Firm*, Alan Clarke's 1989 television film based loosely on the activities of West Ham's Inter City Firm, is perhaps the most prominent example. The game tended to be depicted by people who didn't feel like football people, who were looking at it from the outside with distaste and appalled fascination. And the focuss was exclusively on a tiny sub-culture of violence taken to its logical extreme, as when Gary Oldman's Bexy is shot dead at the end of *The Firm*. Which is fine as far as it goes, but left the vast majority of football fans feeling as though their experience wasn't being represented.

There was a dearth of material looking at football in a lighter vein, a gap that started to be filled by cheaply-produced fanzines, like the gloriously-titled *Brian Moore's Head Looks Uncannily Like London Planetarium*, which was devoted to Gillingham. I met Brian Moore once, when he did some superlative fake commentary for my television comedy *Bostock's Cup*, and I found myself mentally checking his impressive dome, I couldn't help it.

Many clubs had their equivalents – Oldham's was called *Beyond the Boundary* – and they tended to take an irreverent view which sometimes brought them into conflict with those who ran the clubs that were the object of the writers' devotion. They would typically be sold outside the ground by their enthusiastic progenitors, just along the street from the club's over-priced programme offering. And they would sell just as well to away fans, keen for a cheap and cheerful insight into the world-view of that week's opposition.

The daddy of them all was aimed at everyone; it was literate, witty, and took football seriously. *When Saturday Comes* started in 1986, with its distinctive Private Eye-like speech bubble front covers. By 1988 it had gone from a small independently-produced mag to a publication that was available in newsagents across the country.

After Italia 90, the penalties and Gazza's emotional breakdown in front of 26.2 million viewers, it seemed like it was suddenly all right to be a football fan again. It was as though football itself had been redeemed by a martyr's tears.

Pretty soon you could hardly call yourself a celebrity unless you had some sort of lifelong (i.e. for the rest of your life, starting now) allegiance to some football club or other. If you were canny about it, you'd attach yourself to a club that was likely to feature in the latter stages of cup competitions, because more and more now that would provide openings for high-profile guest appearances, little puff pieces on *Football Focus* and the like.

The time was more or less ripe for something about the football-watching experience of the vast majority of fans, from the obsessed to the much more casual, who were not represented by the Theatre of Hate approach, and so Arthur Smith and I came up with a play called *An Evening with Gary Lineker*.

When we were asked, as writers more or less constantly are, 'Where do you get your ideas from?' our answer in this case was embarrassingly straightforward. We got the idea for *An Evening with Gary Lineker*, a play about a group of people watching the Italia 90 semi-final in a hotel room in Majorca, from the night we spent in a hotel room in Majorca watching the Italia 90 semi-final with a group of people. That group included Caroline Quentin and Nick Hancock, who both ended up in the play, and our friends Bob Mills and Sarah Howell.

We put the play on in Edinburgh in 1991, where it seemed to strike a chord, and it ended up running in the West End for a year (if you add a couple of short revivals to the first run). Arthur and I found ourselves invited to the Cheltenham Literary Festival along with Nick Hornby, whose *Fever Pitch* was similarly surfing football's new wave of cultural acceptability.

Every night onstage we watched video of the actual match, because we found that if you tried to replace the television picture with, say, a green lightbulb, to provide a similar low-level ambient light to a game, then you just didn't look at it at all, whereas the semi-final drew your eye to it, irresistibly. Which is how I can tell you with some degree of authority what a great game it was, having watched it times without number. At work.

The tide had turned. Where only recently football was box-office and broadcasting poison, now football projects were tumbling over themselves to get to your screen or your bookshelf, or your... well, wherever you keep your theatre ticket stubs.

Fantasy Football leagues became a thing, celebrated (at first, then quietly sidelined) by David Baddiel and Frank Skinner's laddish television show, *Fantasy Football League*. It was set in a kind of replica of the flat the two comics apparently shared, where they were joined by celebrities keen to show off their footy chops in the new landscape, as well as a small number of football fans dutifully wearing their clubs' replikits who provided chanting and cheering (and much laughter) in the way that small numbers of fans do, where they try to make their voices sound like a much larger crowd by blurring their diction and not hitting the notes of any song they attempt.

Elton John's Glasses, a comedy play about Watford, made it to the West End, and Andrew Lloyd Webber collaborated with Ben Elton – by mistake, according to David Baddiel's hilarious stand-up show – to produce a musical called *The Beautiful Game*.

Then there was *The Manageress*, in which Cherie Lunghi's leading character was so far ahead of her time that her time hasn't even arrived yet, a bit like Captain Kirk.

Sky had a series called *Dream Team* with some clever recolouring of live action to fit in with their fictional team's purple kit. The fictional team was called Harchester United, barely half a side-step from Roy Race's Melchester Rovers. They also had a sort of reality boot camp show called *The Match*, in which celebrities went into training with former England boss Graham Taylor to prepare for a showdown against a team of ex-pros. The celebrities ranged from soap stars like Tom Craig, sitcom stars like Ralf Little, to blokes who are friends of Robbie Williams like Jonathan Wilkes, scorer of the Celebs' only ever goal in three series, when his cross-cum-shot floated over Peter Bonetti.

There was a film of *Fever Pitch*, starring Colin Firth. We made a television film of *An Evening with Gary Lineker*, starring Clive Owen, Caroline Quentin and Martin Clunes, which was set on Ibiza rather than Majorca because the producer (Andy Harries, who later made the excellent *Damned United*) got the use of Rod Stewart's villa there as the set. Arthur wrote a sort of follow-up about Euro 96 called *My Summer with Des*, and I wrote a spoof called *Bostock's Cup* about a third division club winning the FA Cup in 1974. It was on ITV, who never repeat anything and who refuse to consider releasing it on DVD, but the whole thing is on YouTube if you want to check it out.

When Saturday Comes expanded into an established part of the magazine publishing landscape. And then pretty soon there was *FourFourTwo*, a full-fledged grown-up glossy magazine devoted to all things football, where previously all the mainstream mags had really been for kids, such as *Shoot*, *Match* and *Roy of the Rovers*.

Where there was rehabilitation, of course, there was commercial opportunity, and alongside all this cultural rejuvenation, feeding it, living off it, exploiting the new captive market it revealed, was the biggest change of all...

On
The Premier League

Without a doubt, as Glenn Hoddle (and sometimes Jamie Red-knapp and Frank Lampard) is over-fond of saying, the beginning of the Premier League is a massive milestone in the history of modern English football. Maybe even the biggest one of all.

Nowadays, a quarter of a century further down the road, it seems almost as if that is where football history itself began. It's like the moment B.C. became A.D. – in terms of its being a really important date with a definite before-and-after feel to it, I mean, not because it is as significant as the birth of the baby Jesus. I wouldn't want to open that can of worms.

Just look at Gary Lineker and Alan Shearer on any given *Match of the Day*, when Harry Kane (let's say) has just become the youngest person to do something or other in 'the history of the Premiership'. It's like that is when football began. And Shearer sits there with his big grin, knowing that he is the highest goal scorer in 'the history of the Premiership', whilst poor old Gary Lineker, who retired in 1992 (apart from the time he spent in Japan, which is pretty much the same thing) never played a single game or scored a single goal in the Premiership era. It's like every week he is forced to admit that really his whole career counted for nothing.

So how did it come about, this Premier League (or Premiership, depending on who was sponsoring it at the time)?

In 1990 the time felt right for a change. Italia 90 had made football palatable again to a public that before that tournament had mostly viewed it with distaste. Gazza's magical tears had bathed football, washed it clean, and made it seem like a market-friendly commodity once again. Television was only going to be wanting more, and the most recent negotiation a couple of years before had seen the price of rights go from £6 million to £44 million as ITV tried to blow the Beeb out of the water. That bonanza was paid to the Football League, and distributed all the way down through the 92 clubs. The big clubs thought they should be getting a bigger slice of the bumper cake – after all they were the headline acts – and there had been some half-arsed grumbling about Super Leagues without anyone ever really thinking that was anything more than a negotiating tactic.

In January of 1990 the Taylor Report into the Hillsborough Disaster contained the recommendation that major stadia should be converted to all-seater venues. Lord Justice Taylor didn't say that standing was necessarily unsafe, but it had clearly been a factor of sorts in the events of April 1989, even if the main reason was found to be the failure of police control. The Football League brought in regulations that required the clubs in the top two divisions to comply with the recommendations of the Taylor Report by August 1994. This was going to mean a lot of major construction work for everyone. And all that was going to cost a bob or two.

Now all this could have been handled in such a way that it didn't create a gulf, a yawning black chasm really, between the top echelon and the also-rans. In a way that retained the integrity of the structure of English football, that retained the possibility that any team, however impecunious or humble, could have a season like Oldham had in 1989-90, or could do what Northampton Town did in the 1960s when they got promoted from Division Four to Division One (and then slid all the way back down again). It could have been handled in a way that didn't turn football into a process where all the clubs in the country arranged themselves roughly in financial order year after year, in a fashion reminiscent of the most tedious of eight-month-long Grands Prix, with only the freak performance of (actually phenomenally wealthy: see p.207) Leicester City to point at as if to say the magic still happens.

But it wasn't. And the reasons why it wasn't go back to the middle of the century before last.

The Football League vs the Football Association

The historic antipathy between the Football League and the Football Association had its roots in the previous century, and in the contrasting origins of the two organisations. The Football Association was born in 1863, smack in the middle of the Victorian era. There was a great belief at the time in the efficacy of sport, both for reasons of public health and public order, and several prominent Victorians took it upon themselves to codify sports and organise them into proper competitions. Lawn tennis was one sport that acquired its definitive rules in this period; we were not far off the first cricket test match; and the Marquess of Queensberry was about to bring three-minute rounds, sportsmanship and – perhaps most importantly of all – gloves to boxing.

At that time there were almost as many different sets of rules as there were schools that played the game, although there were a couple of systems that were in more widespread use. In the South there were the Cambridge Rules, and in the North another set, called the Sheffield Rules.

The Association was formed with the intention of providing a unified code for the game, and this was cemented in place by their Football Association Cup, which began in 1872. You can get a flavour of the new organisation from the teams that entered those early competitions – Old Etonians, Old Carthusians, Royal Engineers, Clapham Rovers, The Wanderers (not from Wolverhampton). Northern clubs doggedly stuck to their own rules for a few years, but once the F.A. Cup began to be a competition they all wanted to enter, there was a grudging acceptance that the Football Association were now in charge of administering the game for the whole country.

Outside of the F.A. Cup clubs would arrange their own fixtures in a rather chaotic fashion, and dodge the F.A.'s rules against professionalism by finding sneaky ways to pay mercenaries to play for them. Once professionalism was grudgingly permitted by the Southern gentlemen amateurs, the Football League was set up. The Football League was made up of clubs from the Midlands and the North, and its 12 member clubs played each other home and away. The first season was 1888-89, and the first champions were Preston North End, who then rather rubbed the F.A.'s noses in it by winning the Cup as well. Professional Football League clubs soon dominated the F.A.'s own competition, and set up a Second Division to include more clubs that were desperate to join in.

All these Football League clubs were members of the Football Association and subject to its rules, but gallingly the competition that came to dominate the footballing landscape – the League – was not organised by them, and a rancorous antipathy grew between the hardened Northern professionals and the dilettante Southern amateurs.

The Association had to content itself with the Cup, with running all the subsidiary County F.A.s – each of which needed tickets for the Cup Final, of course – and with the national team. The Association represented English football internationally when it came to dealings with UEFA and FIFA, but whenever it tried to suggest changes that would benefit the national team – that elderly canard, the winter break, for instance – they would find the Football League digging its metaphorical heels in, since it operated solely for the benefit of its member clubs.

The loggerheads between the League in Lytham St Annes and the F.A. at Lancaster Gate in London had existed for well over a century by the time the Premier League breakaway was mooted, and you can only imagine the glee with which F.A. hands were rubbed together...

After dinner, minted

The top clubs in England had threatened to break away several times before the Premier League was seriously mooted. In fact it happened every time there was a television money negotiation, as a way of blackmailing the Football League into handing them the share of an increasingly hungry lion to keep them on board.

They threatened to break away in 1986, wrangling a disproportionate increase in their voting power and a larger share of television and sponsorship money, and then again in 1988 when a ten-team super league was supposedly in the offing, but was forestalled by an even bigger financial appeasement.

The breakaway that would ultimately become the Premier League we know and love/hate to this day was instigated by Greg Dyke, who was then the managing director of LWT, and and his name by saving the ailing TV:AM by taking it careering down-market, introducing Roland Rat – 'the only rat to ever join a sinking ship' – and the Alan Partridge-esque Cooking Canon.

Dyke hosted a secret dinner for representatives of the *soi-disant* Big Five – Manchester United, Liverpool, Everton, Arsenal and Spurs – at which he asked them frankly whether they would be interested in an even larger slice of television rights money. He also asked such equally testing questions as 'Do you want pudding?' and 'Do bears shit in the woods?'

David Dein of Arsenal, an estimable fellow, was deputed to ask the Football Association if they would be prepared to lend some legitimacy to the idea of a breakaway league, and his hand was duly bitten off by a gang of embittered gentlemen who saw a ripe and rosy opportunity to give their historic rivals the bloodiest of bloody noses.

The clubs' chairmen were way too canny to hand over complete control to another established organisation, however, and so the FA Premier League was formed as an entity that was commercially separate from both the F.A. and the Football League, able to negotiate its own sponsorship and television deals.

When it came to it, poor old Greg Dyke and LWT missed out entirely, despite having hosted the dinner that kicked the whole thing off. The bidding war was won by BskyB, who had moulds of their own to smash, with the BBC winning rights to show highlights so that they could revive their perennially popular *Match of the Day* programme.

BskyB were forking out an almost unbelievable £304 million, where the previous deal had been with ITV for £44 million, and the one before that was for just £6 million. Money was going to start pouring into the game and would change things for ever.

So it began

The Football League, as it happened, had been in a state of flux over the previous few seasons. Play-offs were brought in for 1986-87 (just in time for Oldham to be the first third-placed team to miss out on automatic promotion to the First Division). The First Division had been reduced to 20 teams over the course of a couple of seasons, then returned to 22 teams for 1991-92. Meanwhile there was a plan to increase the long-established 92 complement to 93 and then 94, but that plan foundered when first Aldershot then Maidstone United went bust and dropped out.

So during the 1991-92 season the 22 First Division clubs all resigned from the Football League to found the FA Premier League. Those 22 clubs were as follows: Arsenal, Aston Villa, Chelsea, Coventry City, Crystal Palace, Everton, Leeds United, Liverpool, Luton Town, Manchester City, Manchester United, Norwich City, Nottingham Forest, Notts County, Oldham Athletic, Queens Park Rangers, Sheffield United, Sheffield Wednesday, Southampton, Tottenham Hotspur, West Ham United and Wimbledon.

There was an agreement to continue promotion out of and relegation into the Football League, so Blackburn Rovers, Ipswich Town and Middlesbrough took part in the inaugural season, replacing the unfortunate Luton, Notts County and West Ham, the turkeys who discovered they had voted for Christmas.

It's hard to establish a new brand, especially when it is in nearly every respect the same as the old brand except that you have found a way of screwing more money out of everyone concerned, and it doesn't help when after one season you change the name of it again. Still, this was a 'whole new ball game' (© BSkyB), and when Carling came aboard as sponsors they decided it was going to be a Premiership, rather than a Premier League. It remained the FA Carling Premiership until 2001, when it rebranded again as the Barclaycard Premiership. Then (2004-07) the FA Barclays Premiership, until the golden goose had become so well established that they didn't need the FA to legitimise it any longer and they styled themselves simply the Barclays Premier League. Since 2016 there has been no main sponsor. They say they want to retain the purity of the brand by just being the Premier League from now on, or even worse, the EPL, but I bet they've just priced themselves out of being sponsored by anyone except Facebook, and that would just alienate too many people (and give fuel to the sneaking suspicion that Russia was now running the whole thing).

To try and sell the nation this pup in the first place, the F.A. claimed that it would be in the interests of the England team. They would see to it that the Premier League was reduced to twenty teams, and thus the players would be less exhausted by the rigours of the season. This indeed came to pass in 1995, a time when UEFA was pressuring all the top leagues – Serie A, the Bundesliga, La Liga, and our one – to reduce to eighteen teams for the good of international footballers everywhere. The Premiership, however, was not interested in voting to kick another two of its members off the gravy train, with the attendant difficulties in getting back on board, so that was firmly resisted. So much for it being good for England.

So the chairmen of the self-styled elite clubs finally bit the bullet and did what they had always dreamed of doing, and they cut themselves loose from the dead weight of the rest of the 92 Club. You can't really blame them, in a way, because their jobs were to do what was best for their one single club, not for the game as a whole. They were businessmen, not romantics. It should have been somebody else's job to take a larger view and make sure that the integrity of the game remained intact.

It was somebody else's job. They just didn't do it.

And that was a great big juicy bit of football's soul that was sold, right there.

On
Murdoch

If football can be said to have sold its soul, then there's not much debate as to the identity of the devil that acquired it. Rupert Murdoch was synonymous with *The Sun*, the populist tabloid that brought us topless Page Three girls even as it took the piss out of them – 'Kelly-Marie, 19, is from Romford, and she thinks Britain should leave the Exchange Rate Mechanism before the recession gets any worse'. It also, let us not forget, brought us 'Freddie Starr Ate My Hamster', the lowest-common-denominator sensibilities of Kelvin McKenzie, and a crowing, bragging certainty that it was able to decide the results of successive General Elections – 'It Was *The Sun* Wot Done It!' – keeping the Tories in power until Tony Blair was able to debase himself sufficiently to turn the tide.

Murdoch's News International first ventured into satellite broadcasting in 1983 when it became the majority shareholder of a pan-European service called, in a Ronseal sort of a way, Satellite Television. This was renamed Sky Channel in 1984, and became the four-channel Sky Television in 1988. Murdoch lost out on a franchise to broadcast in the UK to British Satellite Broadcasting, run by a consortium of Granada, Anglia, Virgin, Pearson, ITN and Alan Sugar's Amstrad. I actually did some comedy sketches for BSB back in the day, which I strongly suspect were seen by nobody at all, not even me.

After BSB launched in 1990 both it and Sky found great difficulty in persuading people to sign up and stick either the round Sky dish or the BSB 'squarial' on their rooves. The two outfits merged in November to become BskyB, much as a mackerel will merge with a shark to form a slightly fuller shark.

The takeover – sorry, merger – caused some serious indigestion problems for Murdoch. The new company was quickly losing something like £14 million a week. Mooted fixes ranged from to throwing everything behind a subscription movie channel, which would require extensive and unappealing negotiations with distributors, to just showing pornography, which risked putting an end to page 3 once and for all, to – option C – offering exclusive access to sports via a pay-per-view sports channel.

BSkyB already had some cricket and some rugby league and now it set its sights on the Premier League, which was in the process of setting up and ready to negotiate its first television deal.

ITV were the current rights holders, but their deal was with the old Football League. Many of the new Premier League chairmen were known to be unhappy with the way ITV only seemed interested in Big Five games. However, David Dein, the Arsenal chairman, clearly favoured doing business with Greg Dyke, and apparently discussed the possibility of ITV doing deals with the clubs individually for rights.

When it came to the vote, ITV had made a colossal bid by

previous standards of £262 million for 30 live games a season. BSkyB blew this out of the water with a £304 million bid for 60 live games a season.

Despite David Dein's concerns about BSkyB's £2 billion debt, and whether they would ever even see a penny of this monster offer, the count was 14-6 (two bold and decisive club chairmen abstained), with Liverpool, Manchester United, Everton and Arsenal among the half dozen backing ITV's bid. Amusingly, this meant that four of the Big Five still didn't get their way despite going to all the trouble of trying to make small talk round at Greg Dyke's without mentioning Roland Rat.

Of course, it would have been tricky for Liverpool to favour the BSkyB option, given the rancorous reaction to Murdoch's *Sun* in the wake of its outrageous slurs on the city and its people at the time of the Hillsborough tragedy. The headline 'The Truth' had appeared above entirely fabricated stories about Liverpool fans urinating on and beating up policemen, and picking the pockets of the victims.

In effect, then, the rump of the Premier League plumped for Murdoch, and he suddenly had the licence to shape football to suit his own commercial ends. The sweetener, as far as football fans were concerned, was that the deal also involved the return of *Match of the Day*, as BBC were in cahoots with BSkyB for the highlights package.

Murdoch described football as the 'battering ram' with which he would smash his way into the households of Britain. He certainly battered his way into our household, although perhaps not through the front door. A young nephew won a Sky dish and system in a newspaper competition, and as Oldham were then still in the Premiership I persuaded him to swap it for a cuddly dinosaur, a deal which the young man, now a top web-designing computer programmer in his thirties, still views with some bitterness these many years later.

And so as fans who attended matches were having to get used to a new way of watching, what with the top two divisions committed to converting their stadia to an all-seater set up, so armchair fans too were having to adjust, as now there were going to be sixty live games a year for the next five years to digest. Which seemed like an awful lot.

Still, at least *Match of the Day* was back.

How we used to watch football on the telly before there was Sky

When I was a lad and first becoming obsessed with football it was far from a wall-to-wall prime time entertainment. If you wanted to watch football on television you had to seek it out in its late-night or Sunday-afternoon backwaters. *Match of the Day* was the big treat, of course, on a Saturday night after the main news – which would evince no sympathy for the viewer who had tried not to hear the score of the two featured games so as to have at least a small taste of the live match experience.

It was a hardy soul indeed who would try to make it all the way to *Football Special* the following afternoon without knowing the score of the regional main match, which was different depending on where you were in the country. My parents lived near Sheffield, so we would get the Yorkshire TV version, hosted by Fred Dinenage with commentary by Keith Macklin or fledgling superstar Martin Tyler. It was a Leeds United game two weeks out of three in those days I'd guess, with occasional air-time for the Sheffield United of the Alan Woodward vintage, or the Hull City of Ken Wagstaff, or Tommy Craig's Sheffield Wednesday in their 'blue Arsenal' strip, or even York City, promoted above their wildest dreams and playing in a brown kit with a big white Y on the front.

Sometimes, if the weather was propitious, we could pick up a fuzzy signal from a midlands-based transmitter, and see some of ATV's Sunday afternoon highlights.

In midweek, if we were lucky, *Sportsnight with Coleman* would feature some action from a European tie featuring an English side away in Bulgaria or something like that. Again, you could indulge in Likely Lad-style antics to try and keep an extra little edge, but often the highlights would be brief and then Coleman would be switching to athletics or some such, and your midweek fix was done.

As for live matches...

The F.A. Cup final was the big live football television event of the season, which is why the 1970s and early 1980s finals are so memorable to the generation that watched them. There would be hours of build-up, which would include things like *Cup Final It's a Knockout*, in which two teams of fans from the participating clubs would compete in giant foam costumes, or *Cup Final Question of Sport* featuring players from each side.

Sometimes we would be privy to some of the teams' preparation. I vividly remember the Watford players filmed having breakfast before the 1984 final, while Michael Barrymore (a popular entertainer of the day) clowned around blacked-up like a golliwog pretending to be John Barnes (different times – although sometimes shrugging and saying 'different times' doesn't actually cut it. I still remember the carpet burn as my jaw hit the floor back then, 34 years ago). Then cameras would be on the coach heading for Wembley, hearing about how many members of Everton full back John Bailey's family were going to be at the game (in the region of thirty), or marvelling at Kenny Sansom's impression of Norman Wisdom (Mister Grimsdale!)

The Cup Final was huge. I remember the pilgrimages we would make to a friend's grandparents' house in Rotherham, because they were the only people we knew with a colour telly. And after the game we would head out to the park for a kickabout with a migrainous headache from being indoors for nine hours with the curtains drawn, hoovering up every precious second.

Outside of that one regular live football feast, pickings were slim. There would be the Home Internationals, usually the two weekends after the Cup Final. Maybe there would be a mid-week World Cup qualifier that would be deemed important enough to show live. I'm pretty sure that was the case with the key 1973 game against Poland at Wembley, but I can't be one hundred percent sure.

What I do know is that my bond with football was created and strengthened by its very scarcity. When I was a kid we had to take what little was on offer, observe the precious time-slots with religious fervour, and if we wanted to see live football, well, by and large we had to go to a game.

Now kids were going to be presented with live games every Sunday – a Super Sunday, no less – and on a Monday evening. They were going to get a proper surfeit of Richard Keys and Andy Gray, they were going to see cheerleaders and fireworks as the new broadcaster tried to gild the lily, and they were going to watch a couple of idiots in foam rubber suits bumping into one another in the centre circle – not just once a year in the Cup Final build-up but every single week – as the commentator, maybe even Martin Tyler, assured them despite all evidence to the contrary that 'Everyone loves the sumos!'

A whole new ball game indeed.

On
Bosman

Supposing you had to come up with the name of the single player who has been most instrumental in making the game the way it is today – who would you come up with? Cristiano Ronaldo? Pep Guardiola? Original Ronaldo? Diego Maradona? Johan Cruyff? Jimmy Hill, even?

I think you could make a pretty good case for an obscure Belgian player from the early 1990s. You may not know too much about his playing career, but you will know his name – his surname, at least.

Jean-Marc Bosman was playing for RFC Liege in the Belgian First Division when he reached the end of his contract in 1990. He was offered a greatly reduced deal, as he hadn't been making the first team, and decided he wanted to move on to play for Dunkerque in France. RFC Liege still held his registration, however, and under the system then in place this meant that they could demand a transfer fee. Dunkerque couldn't afford the asking price, Bosman refused to sign his new contract and was then suspended.

Bosman lawyered up and took RFC Liege, the Belgian FA and UEFA to the European Court of Justice in Luxembourg claiming all this amounted to restraint of trade, and changed football forever, to the extent that recent history can be neatly divided into two eras – pre-Bosman and post-Bosman.

It took a while for the legal wheels to grind, but finally in December 1995 the court ruled that the player registration system placed a restriction on the free movement of workers that was prohibited by the terms of the EC Treaty.

The Bosman Ruling, as it became known, meant that players could move to a new club at the end of their contract without their previous employer receiving any kind of fee.

Pre-post

Pre-Bosman a player could not leave at the end of his deal unless his club agreed to let him go on a free, or that club received an agreed transfer fee from a buying club to purchase the player's registration.

This meant the power rested entirely with the clubs. Being a footballer simply wasn't like any other job. A footballer, for all the undoubted perks, was bound by what Bosman himself described as 'transfer slavery'. The club effectively owned their player as an asset.

Suddenly, post-Bosman, players realised that the power now rested with them. More particularly, with a new breed of ball-busting agents who were prepared to play hardball with employers, and agitate to move their clients on again via ever-more lucrative deals almost as soon as they had completed the obligatory arrival photo with either scarf over head or new shirt with name and number.

As an extra unforeseen consequence, the Bosman Ruling

prohibited UEFA and the various domestic leagues under its aegis from operating any kind of quota system for so-called foreign players, as this was also restricting the free movement of labour.

When the Premier League began in 1992 there were just eleven foreign players on the rosters of the 22 clubs. By the tenth anniversary of the Bosman Ruling foreign mercenaries made up 50 percent of the top tier squads, and nowadays it's more like 70 percent.

Pre-Bosman, clubs taking part in European club competitions could only field three foreign players, plus two more if they had progressed through the team's academy system. In 1994, as a result of UEFA's counting Welsh and Scottish players as foreign to English sides, along with the Irish, of course, Alex Ferguson had to replace Peter Schmeichel with Gary Walsh for a game against Barcelona at the Nou Camp in order to squeeze in Andrei Kanchelskis, Denis Irwin, Roy Keane, Ryan Giggs and Mark Hughes – they lost 4-0.

Post-Bosman the top clubs could play as many EU players as they liked, and United returned to the Nou Camp in 1999 to lift the trophy with eight foreigners in their team, including match-winning super-sub Ole Gunnar Solskjaer.

Worth the paper it's printed on?

The post-Bosman free-for-all coincided with football becoming awash with money, the Murdoch millions – billions, actually (that still works if you say Murdoch's name while pretending to have a quite severe head cold). But did that period coincide with a generous-spirited trickle-down through the whole football league system guaranteeing the robust health of all 92 clubs? Did it go towards a warm-hearted reduction in ticket prices for fans who wanted to watch games live and contribute to the atmosphere so prized by the broadcasters?

Of course not, because the top players and their agents quickly realised that the sky was the limit for wages, signing-on fees, loyalty bonuses (ha!) and the occasional old-style transfer of a star player for eye-wateringly exorbitant amounts, because no club dared fall off the runaway gravy train because they'd never be able to catch it up again. So a huge proportion of that incredible windfall simply left the game, going into agents' pockets – £211 million was paid to agents last year alone – and towards players' mansions, sports cars, diamond-encrusted watches and huge meaningless fines for arbitrary offences.

The transfer system became a ransom system, pure and simple, where top players gravitate inexorably to the handfuls of top clubs in the richest leagues, and those top few clubs dominate their domestic competitions and the Champions League year after year after year.

The gulf between the elite clubs and the rest has never been wider. Smaller clubs used to be able to keep afloat financially by operating a youth or academy system that 'found' and developed promising youngsters into saleable assets. Crewe is often held up as an example, despite the shadow that has been cast over that operation recently, Post-Bosman this revenue stream was severely compromised. Smaller clubs risked losing players they had spent years developing for next to nothing, or having to cash in much earlier than they would like to.

Once upon a more sensible time it was the norm for a player to learn his trade in the lower leagues, before maybe getting the chance to earn himself and his parent club a bigger payday once he was deemed ready to step up. Now it is much harder to hang onto these kids, especially once a fledgling's head has been turned by the prospect of earning a small fortune for sitting on the sub's bench at Chelsea for a season before being loaned out to an obscure Belgian second division side and never being heard of again.

The one – the only – thing the football authorities managed to do to mitigate this without upsetting the EU Court was to introduce a scheme whereby a developing club would be due a fee for losing a player to a head-turning offer before the age of 24. This is often decided by a tribunal, however, so there's little chance of being able to hold the big boys to ransom, not like the super agents can.

Players' contracts have become increasingly absurd, since the Bosman Ruling gave stars the right to start talking to other employers in the last six months of the deal. Effectively this has come to mean that a two-year deal is really a one-year deal, because with twelve months to go renegotiations have to begin so that clubs can forestall the possibility of losing an asset for nothing at the end of the contract.

There was the extraordinary scenario at Arsenal in the summer of 2017, where the club's two star players, Mesut Ozil and Alexis Sanchez, both entered the last twelve months of their contracts. Boss Arsene Wenger didn't want to lose them, and they were contracted to play for him for another season, but the club stood to lose millions if the stars ran their contracts down and left for free at the end of them. At first Wenger seemed to have won the argument and started the 2017-18 season with the two players in his squad. Both were below par, though, unsettled by uncertainty and the huge sums being dangled before their eyes, and before long Sanchez had been cashed in on and had taken his poor form up to Old Trafford, while Ozil agreed a new deal to stay where he was. The upshot being that

Sanchez and Ozil are at time of writing the two most highly-paid footballers in the game, with Sanchez's contract worth an eye-popping £25 million a year.

Consequences

So Bosman is responsible for many far-reaching consequences, by no means all intended.

Top of the list: players have all the power now, and have been able to bleed a vast proportion of the television bonanza out of the clubs and out of the game altogether.

The more expensive players become, the more the advantage lies with a super elite of clubs, the top handful in each of the most lucrative leagues in Europe. The richest clubs become even richer, and poorer clubs are forced ever closer to the bread line.

The super-rich Premier League is awash with foreign mercenaries, meaning that every year Gareth Southgate or whoever else is doing the Impossible Job has fewer and fewer options to choose from.

Even though transfer activity being limited to two windows per year, our back pages are nevertheless filled with speculation about whether players will be negotiating new deals – or not – even though they are already earning more in a week than some of their fans will see in a lifetime.

Football as a whole has never come up with an adequate fix for this – somewhere halfway between the old registration and transfer system and the post-Bosman free-for-all. There were noises. In 2005 UEFA declared its intention to do something to repair the damage, but talks with the EU came to nothing.

After Brexit, perhaps EU freedom of movement regulations won't carry quite the weight they did back in the 1990s, although the post-Bosman way of doing things seems pretty entrenched both inside and outside the EU nowadays, so perhaps that mangy malnourished horse has bolted.

Or has it?

Post-Bosman Post-Brexit

At the time of writing the Premier League clubs are all a bit agitated about Brexit. It's not clear, you see, how that ill-thought-out national upheaval is going to impact on their ability to take unfair advantage of all the rest of the clubs in the world by using their financial muscle to nick their most promising youngsters. So they keep badgering Theresa May about what her plan – in the loosest possible sense of the word – might mean for the future employment of EU nationals. But she, a true watered-down clone of Margaret Thatcher, has no real interest in football, having never even claimed to support a team which she can then get wrong in a speech, like her gammon-faced predecessor.

It could be that post-Brexit Britain will subject players from the European Economic Area to the same regulations it currently applies to those from outside the EU. This would mean work permits would only be issued if the player in question has played a certain quota of his country's international games in the past two years – this percentage varies according to FIFA's idiosyncratic world rankings – or commands a fee in excess of the ever-upward-spiralling Premier League median. In addition the player would have to be over 18, so there'd be no more of the sort of inspired cradle-snatching that brought Cesc Fabregas, for example, or Nicolas Anelka, or Gerard Pique or the first version of Paul Pogba to England, not to mention about a third of Chelsea's vast playing staff, most of whom seem to be currently on indefinite loans to clubs in Belgium.

Among the recent players who would not have been able to come to our Premier League are several who have actually won it, including most notably N'Golo Kante, Riyad Mahrez and Robert Huth, the spine of the Leicester 'miracle'.

The Premier League bleats that any change in how they are able to operate in the international transfer market risks diluting one of the UK's most successful exports, and diminishing our country's profile on the international stage.

Whisper this, though: if they are no longer able to stuff their squads with quick-fix second-level foreigners won't this mean that the ones who do come here will all be of a higher quality? They will still come, of course they will, because the Premier League is a fantastical money tree. And then won't the big clubs be obliged to actually get serious about bringing through their own players, which would be good? And might they not also have to start uncovering gems in the lower leagues, and start actually filtering some of their improbable billions down into English football? And wouldn't both of those things be… good things?

Perhaps Theresa May should consider being as strict as she can with the Premier League, because football fans elsewhere might actually help her nick a second referendum if that comes.

Jean-Marc lui-même

Jean-Marc Bosman never really managed to pick up his football career during or after his lengthy court action.

Bosman hoped that players who benefitted from his legal stand would support him by buying and wearing his line of 'Who's the Boz?' T-shirts, but he later mournfully claimed to have sold only one, and that one was to the son of his own lawyer.

Whatever, Bosman regards himself as a kind of heroic martyr, and whenever you see him interviewed he is chuntering on about how Cristiano Ronaldo owes him everything, and muttering darkly about how ungrateful stars should turn out for some kind of testimonial game for him. Good luck with that, is what I say.

Cristiano Ronaldo doesn't strike me as a man who believes he owes anyone anything, and most people outside of football would regard the substantial compensation cheque Bosman received after the court case as more than adequate to allow him to stop banging on about it, even if it would only buy him a week and a half of Alexei Sanchez's services at today's post-Bosman going rate.

On the other hand, Ronaldo bought his agent an island.

On
Football's Coming Home

There was great excitement as Euro 96 loomed. The first tournament to take place on English soil for thirty years, and we all knew what happened last time, so surely a home victory was on the cards. Yet in truth England hadn't built on their great run to the semi-final of Italia 90, not at all. Of course, they had reduced the chance of that happening by dispensing with the services of the manager who had achieved it, but surely in Paul Gascoigne we had discovered a player that we could build a team around for years to come.

Well, Graham Taylor, the new England manager, didn't think so. Pretty much his first order of business was to drop Gazza in favour of 32-year-old Gordon Cowans, a useful player no doubt, but unlikely to be dubbed Gozza any time soon. Taylor said that there were tactical reasons for leaving out his star player, who was in fine form and well on the way to being named Footballer of the Year, but there was a strong suspicion that Taylor was simply no good at handling big-name stars. Which is pretty much what the England job mostly involves.

One small piece of insight I can offer comes from the spring of 1992. I was acting in *An Evening with Gary Lineker* at the time. Gary came to see the show a couple of times, and said that he would suggest to Graham Taylor that he bring the England squad along next time there was a squad get-together for a friendly. They often went on theatre outings, apparently, and had recently been to see *Buddy* (more cricket than football).

This visit was duly set up, but then it was cancelled, then on again, then off. We had the strong impression that Taylor was opposed to it, partly because it wasn't his idea and partly because the evening was all about Gary. Anyway, just before the performance in question the England luxury coach pulled up outside the theatre, and the squad jogged into the building, across the lobby and down into the stalls to take their seats without pausing to interact with anyone. You could almost see the white board, hear Taylor preparing them for the ordeal ahead, leaving nothing to chance. He sat at the back, many rows behind them, with Peter Bonetti and Alan Ball, like schoolteachers keeping an eye on an unruly school trip. It was hard to see why Taylor had made such a meal out of the whole thing, unless he was just really insecure and felt threatened by Lineker's status.

Gazza wasn't there. He'd crocked himself in the 1991 Cup Final tackling Nottingham Forest's Gary Charles, having just completed a move to Lazio for £8.5 million that Spurs manager Terry Venables described as 'like watching your mother-in-law drive off a cliff in your new car'. Not altogether sure what he meant by that, to be honest.

England had qualified unconvincingly for Euro 92, where they played out two goalless draws against France and Denmark, and then lost to Sweden. The most memorable part of the whole debacle was that Taylor hauled Gary Lineker off when England were trailing Sweden and desperately needed a goal, a wrong-headed decision that lost him whatever sympathy he might have come home to, and probably says more about their relationship than it does about the football. *The Sun*'s headline the next morning was 'Swedes 2, Turnips 1', and that really kicked off the tabloid's campaign to oust him.

Denmark won the thing, having only been invited along at the last moment when Yugoslavia, who'd qualified ahead of them, dissolved into civil war and stopped being a country any more.

The 1994 World Cup was in the United States, with FIFA's collective eyes having lit up at the thought of broaching the richest commercial marketplace in the world. Of course there was not much of an organised game over there as tournaments and franchises seemed to come and go, and not many stadia that would pass muster, but never mind, they would be built, and lucrative construction contracts could be wrangled over with whatever kickbacks and bonuses could be wrung from the situation.

England's qualification campaign was a disaster, cruelly captured by a Channel Four fly-on-the-wall documentary called *An Impossible Job*. Taylor only had to finish second, which after all was his speciality, but he ended up behind Norway and the Netherlands, with the *coup de grâce* coming after his side conceded a goal after eight seconds at home to San Marino.

Along the way, Taylor was seen flailing around, way out of his depth, and he acquired several rather odd catchphrases. 'Can we not knock it?!' he cried at one point, and of course 'Do I not like that?!' *The Sun* merged his face with a turnip under the headline 'That's Yer Allotment', and Taylor duly resigned.

His replacement was the former Barcelona and Spurs boss Terry Venables (also novelist, singer and nightclub owner), who had been considered for the job in 1990 but ruled out over fears that shady business dealings made him an unsuitable figurehead. After his appointment in January 1994 his probity came under intense scrutiny both in the press and, embarrassingly for everyone, in parliament.

Venables had no qualification concerns for Euro 96 as England were hosts, and he put together some decent results in friendlies – a lot of draws, but still. Bizarrely the F.A. refused to extend his contract until they had seen how his team performed in competitive fixtures, and El Tel decided he would stand down after the tournament. Glenn Hoddle was appointed before the shindig kicked off, in an eerie echo of the shambolic way the F.A. had mishandled the build-up to Italia 90.

Of course, that was not the only parallel with the earlier tournament. England drew their first game, as they had then, and came under criticism from an impatient tabloid press. Then, however, they beat Scotland 2-0, with a stellar goal from Paul Gascoigne, which he celebrated by mimicking the 'dentist's chair', a drinking game that had brought the squad some self-righteously critical pre-tournament press coverage. They followed with a brilliant performance against the Netherlands, who they blew away 4-1, with Alan Shearer and Teddy Sheringham outstanding together up front.

Spain were next in the quarter-finals, and we beat them in a penalty shoot-out – we didn't know that we were cursed in them yet – with Stuart Pearce exorcising the demons of six years before by slamming his home and then roaring with demented vindication, all the veins standing out on his neck.

Pearce hadn't been in the squad that came to *An Evening*

with Gary Lineker, where he would have been faced with reliving the worst moment of his life. Nigel Clough, his Nottingham Forest team-mate, was there, though, and he dragged old Psycho along to see the show when it came to Nottingham on tour. Everyone in the theatre knew he was there, of course, and as the crucial penalty approached all eyes were on him as he clenched the arms of his seat, knuckles white, emotions raw. What Nigel Clough knew, of course, was that in the play Pearce's penalty is the point at which a flight of fantasy into an alternate reality begins. Apparently, when the character onstage cried 'Pearce... *scores!*' the great man thrust his fists into the air and did 'the face' – the one he did in 1996 when he scored his penalty against Spain. Top man.

The Germans lay in wait in the semi, as they had six years before. On that sunny evening the television cameras picked out David Baddiel and Frank Skinner, beaming in disbelieving pride as the whole crowd roared out 'It's coming home, it's coming home, it's coming... Football's coming home!' – the unstoppable anthem of that summer (and some subsequent ones, as it turned out) that they had created with the Lightning Seeds.

As six years before, it was a brilliant game of football. Shearer scored early, Stefan Kuntz equalised soon after. The match went into golden goal extra time, in which Germany had a goal disallowed, Darren Anderton hit the post, and Paul Gascoigne came agonisingly close to sliding in a low Shearer cross across the six-yard box.

It went to penalties, and both sides dispatched the first five with ruthless efficiency. Gareth Southgate found himself taking the first of the sudden death kicks, and scuffed it tamely to the keeper Andreas Kopke. Andreas Moller stuck the winning kick in, and the Germans went on to beat the Czech Republic in the final.

As in 1990 it had been a terrific, thrilling ride. Once again, though, England found themselves back at square one, having once again undermined and stuffed up the continuity on the management side of things. It's one thing to keep making mistakes, it's another not to ever learn from them.

On
Things Can Only Get Better

'Things can only get better' was the bouncy anthem of 1997 as Tony Blair's (New) Labour swept to power. And 1997 was also the year that Rupert Murdoch's first five-year deal to broadcast the Premiership ran out.

Tactically, stylistically, the game had remained more or less the same after the big bang. It was still the sort of high-energy, blood-and-thunder offering that the rest of football civilisation turned its nose up at – although there were certainly a lot more foreign players playing in England, as the Premiership clubs began to flex their financial muscle.

When the Premier League kicked off in 1992 there were just 13 foreigners involved in the action. You could only have made them into a team by playing one of the four goalkeepers at centre back – Peter Schmeichel, perhaps – but you'd have had Eric Cantona up front so you'd have had a chance of scoring a goal or two, as long as he wasn't laying the chances on for Ronnie Rosenthal, Liverpool's Israeli crossbar king.

There were Scandinavians, like Oldham's Gunnar Halle,

Sheffield Wednesday's Roland Nilsson and Anders Limpar and John Jensen at Arsenal. There was a Russian (Andrei Kanchelskis), a couple of Dutchmen (Michel Vonk and Hans Segers), a Pole and a Czech (Robert Warzycha and Jan Stejskal) and a Canadian (Craig Forrest).

There were no Germans, no Italians, no Africans, no South Americans and just the one Frenchman, the maverick Cantona, and who knows what he was doing over here? Maybe it was the weather? Certainly there have been few players with such an obvious anxiety about getting sunburn on the back of the neck.

The little burst of enthusiastic enterprise that had brought Ossie Ardiles and Ricky Villa over, and had Harry Haslam trying to snag a young Maradona but ending up with Alex Sabella – that all seemed a long while ago. Mind you, it's not as though there'd been a deal of traffic the other way down the years, as English football was nothing if not determinedly insular.

There had been some successes of course. Kevin Keegan was European Footballer of the Year at Hamburg. Chris Waddle won three French titles at Marseille and was runner-up in their fans' player of the century poll. Gary Lineker did OK at Barcelona, even though they played him on the wing. David Platt played for three Italian clubs, and Glenn Hoddle won the French league at AS Monaco, along with Mark Hateley.

On the flip side, there had been players who'd found it difficult to adjust. Ian Rush had an unhappily homesick season in Italy, which he said was 'like living in a foreign country'.

The influx of talent from beyond our shores really began to pick up momentum in those first few Premiership seasons, and 1997 was the year that foreign players began to outnumber the homegrown members of the top flight squads. By that time we'd started to see some proper international stars illuminating the Premiership – Jurgen Klinsmann, for example, with his self-aware diving celebration. Dennis Bergkamp and Ruud Gullit, Gianluca Vialli and Gianfranco Zola, Patrick Vieira and Emmanuel Petit, Juninho and Faustino Asprilla…

So did Murdoch think the battering ram was working for him? And did the Premiership clubs think the arrangement was satisfactory? Or did they think he needed them more than they needed him? After all, there were other broadcasters out there, maybe someone else would like to capitalise on old Rupert's spadework?

Anyone could see that Murdoch had hung everything, his whole enterprise, on football. Football was getting him into houses, into homes, into the timetable of people's weeks, into the fabric of the nation. They had test match cricket too, of course, and *The Simpsons*, but it was plain to see that it was football that had helped Sky rush past 6 million subscribers.

So when the next block of television rights came up Murdoch had to make absolutely sure that he got them. It was a classic seller's market, and naturally the price went up. He'd originally paid £304 million for his sixty games a year for five years. Now he was obliged to fork out £670 million for the next four.

And the Premiership clubs – who'd been doing just fine already, let's face it – were absolutely rolling in it. More foreign mercenaries were on their way, plenty more, but it wouldn't be a foreign player who would have the biggest impact on how the game evolved over the next few years. It would be a foreign manager.

The Professor

He wasn't the first, strictly speaking. That was Dr Josef Venglos, who took over at Aston Villa when Graham Taylor became

England boss. He lasted a season, unable to put across his suspiciously European ideas about nutrition, recuperation and physiology. Then there were Ossie Ardiles and Ruud Gullit, who were both so well-steeped in the ways of English football from their time as players that they barely registered as a novelty.

Arsène Wenger arrived at Highbury with a degree in economics, a fairly undistinguished playing career, and a vaguely lightweight academic demeanour, and pretty much everyone in football's first thought was, well, no chance.

He seemed to have come from nowhere, although actually he'd been manager of AS Monaco when Glenn Hoddle was there, and also Nagoya Grampus Eight in Japan, which we'd heard of because that's where Gary Lineker went out to pasture.

It wasn't an obvious fit at first. Arsenal were a club with a well-known drinking culture, and such was their dour defending and their expertise at the offside trap that 'One-Nil to the Arsenal' was both a crowd chant and the name of their fanzine.

But maybe it was because the bespectacled owlish Frenchman represented such a culture shock to Arsenal's battle-hardened old pros that he was able to shake them up so comprehensively.

He applied scientific methods to their training sessions, no longer leaving warm-ups to the players themselves, and eradicating lengthy drills designed to boost stamina. In came new methods of stretching, a stopwatch to time every part of training, and ball exercises to sharpen passing skills. He brought in an osteopath and an acupuncturist, and completely rethought the way the players recovered from exertion. They were concerned that they wouldn't be fit enough without having pushed themselves to exhaustion in preparation, but science proved to know what it was talking about.

Wenger also redesigned the players' diets, once he had

got past the early Mars bar revolt, in which senior pros were disgruntled that they no longer got a chocolate treat on match day. Inspired by his time in Japan, he replaced burgers and chips with fish or chicken, mashed potatoes and steamed vegetables. He couldn't stop Tony Adams nipping off to the chip shop after training, but he did support his captain all the way in his ongoing battle with alcoholism, and was rewarded by some stellar performances.

The results of these changes were quickly seen on the pitch. The team that had once taken a perverse pleasure in the nickname 'Boring, boring Arsenal' changed its old focus on rock-like stability and an impregnable offside trap to become a fast-moving attacking side that dominated possession and became the best team to watch in the country.

Wenger supplemented these methods with an equally scientific approach to recruitment. He picked up a 20-year-old French flop from AC Milan and turned him into Patrick Vieira. He bought Nicolas Anelka at 17, and transformed the 22-year-old Thierry Henry into arguably the greatest player the Premiership has seen. He took a keen interest in a player's statistics, in a time before Opta made this information available to everyone.

At Christmas in Wenger's first full season Arsenal were sixth, but then in the spring they won ten games in a row and took the title with two games to spare. Then they beat Newcastle United in the FA Cup final with goals from Overmars and Anelka.

And as if his stock wasn't high enough already, his Monaco protégé Glenn Hoddle was about to take England to a World Cup in France.

The first proper foreign manager was here to stay, and it wasn't long before everyone wanted one. Even England.

It's difficult to imagine now, but in those days there was a feeling that if you wanted a properly successful manager then you really wanted to get yourself a Scottish one. They were old school, they brooked no nonsense, and they just sounded right, somehow.

Alex Ferguson had brought an end to Manchester United's long wait for a First Division title by simply waiting until they called it something else. He won four of the first five Premier Leagues-stroke-Premierships, including twice pulling off the fabled Double (although he needed Mark Hughes to equalise in the last seconds of extra time against Oldham in the 1994 semi to keep the first one on track). This sequence was only interrupted by another Scot, Kenny Dalglish, who had won with Blackburn Rovers in 1995, backed by Jack Walker's millions – the first real indication that the title might ultimately turn out to be purchasable. Dalglish had also won three times as Liverpool manager, alternating with George Graham, who was Scottish, of course, and at that time manager of Arsenal.

Ferguson responded to Wenger's 1997-98 Double with a Treble, which we shall come to shortly, and three titles in a row, but then Wenger won another Double in 2002, and topped that off with a unique invincible season in 2003-04. The rivalry between the pair would define the next decade, at least until Jose Mourinho turned up to stick his oar in.

After Wenger's early successes Tottenham were emboldened to copy Arsenal and try a foreign boss of their own, hiring Swiss coach Christian Gross, the man who brandished a Travelcard at a press conference in an attempt to identify with the fans. When that experiment failed Tottenham went for a Scotsman. Actually, they went for George Graham, the one who used to be at Arsenal in the days before the enlightenment. Funny game, football.

On
The Golden Generation #1

For more than a decade England players and fans suffered under the burden of heightened expectation. We'd reached two semi-finals, albeit with a massive trough in between, and only lost on penalties each time. We were ready to take the next step, ready to push onwards and upwards.

Because, finally, we had a Golden Generation.

When did the idea of a Golden Generation first start to kick in? Perhaps around the time Alan Hansen said that Manchester United wouldn't win the title with the group that came to be called the Class of '92 using the unassailable logic that 'You can't win anything with kids'. Oh yeah? What about the Under-17 World Cup? How else would you go about winning that, Alan?

That had been at the start of the 1995-96 season, and Manchester United went on to win the double. David Beckham, Paul Scholes, Nicky Butt and the Neville brothers, Gary and Phil, seemed to represent an imminent new era of hope for England. A shame that the best of Fergie's crop, Ryan Giggs, was Welsh, but never mind.

All we needed for this bunch to flourish on the international stage was a progressive young manager to take them under his wing. And we had one.

The Hand of Hod

Glenn Hoddle, a stylish playmaker in his day, had taken over the England manager gig after Euro 96.[1] He'd been a player himself not so long ago, indeed he had begun his managerial career as a player-manager at Swindon, where he played himself as a sweeper in a back three, and then he'd continued this attacking style as boss of Chelsea.

It was something of a relief to have a seemingly straightforward football man in charge. The previous couple of years had featured almost as much insinuation about Terry Venables' dodgy business dealings as about his merits as a coach. There seemed always to be hints that there were dark secrets about to come out that would require his immediate sacking. The tabloid press had the scent of England manager blood in their nostrils, having fatally undermined Bobby Robson (eventually) and ridiculed Graham Taylor to extinction, and this was the big stick they were going to beat Venables with. Never mind that the country were delighted to have him in charge, and that football fans bitterly resented this persecution, not giving a flying fuck about what Venables did or didn't do (as long as he promised not to go on chat shows and sing *Bye Bye Blackbird*, a sacking offence if ever I saw one). And after he left, did any real serious dirt come out that would have warranted even a moment's consideration of whether he should be booted out? If so, I don't recall any.

---

1 Though, as previously mentioned, he was appointed before the Euros, thanks to the F.A.'s cack-handed mishandling of the situation, putting Terry Venables' nose out of joint by rolling up to pre-tournament training sessions.

Still, El Tel was gone, and Le Hod (he'd played in France a bit) was in. Hoddle kicked off World Cup qualifying in style with a comfortable 3-0 win in Moldova. He played three at the back, a choice criticised by the still-smarting Venables, but we'd all already moved on.

The game was notable for marking the international debut of David Beckham, and within his first few months the new boss gave debuts to David James, Nicky Butt, Paul Scholes, Rio Ferdinand and Michael Owen (also Andy Hinchcliffe and one-cap wonders Chris Sutton and Lee Hendrie, but still). Combining these newcomers with the established spine that he had inherited – David Seaman, Stuart Pearce, Paul Gascoigne and Alan Shearer – gave England a confident look, and the manager quickly seemed to develop a kind of aura of being the right man in the right job. Clearly he was going to be there for years and years and years…

There was one blip in qualifying, when Hoddle tried to accommodate Matt Le Tissier at home to Italy and lost to a Zola goal. But then in the summer of 1997 England won something called Le Tournoi, a mini-tournament in France, with Paul Scholes in imperious form. They beat France and Italy and lost to Brazil, but still walked off with the trophy, the first thing the senior England side had won since 1966.

And then a gutsy 0-0 draw in Rome, with Gascoigne and Ince outstanding, clinched qualification, and the manager prepared for France 98 with optimism.

Hoddle had demonstrated an impressive level of tactical acumen, but unfortunately his man-management skills were not of a similar standard. He took 28 players to a training camp in La Manga, which meant that before the tournament started six were going to have to be axed. He did this in individual head-to head meetings, and the one where he axed Paul Gascoigne did not go well, despite the soothing strains of Kenny G in the background. Gascoigne trashed the manager's room, and there was widespread shock, despite the fact that the player had clearly not been looking after himself and was struggling to last more than an hour in games.

Then there was the use of Eileen Drewery, a faith healer who'd helped Hoddle during his own playing career, which brought widespread suspicion and ridicule despite the fact that some of the players found her presence useful. Ray Parlour famously requested a short back and sides, and Steve McManaman and Robbie Fowler asked if she knew who would win the 3.15 at Wincanton.

When Teddy Sheringham was on the front pages apparently pissed up in the Algarve, Hoddle sent him out to make a grovelling public apology.

And then he left David Beckham out of the World Cup opener against Tunisia believing he 'lacked focus' because of his burgeoning romance with Spice Girl Victoria Adams. It may have been true, but it made the whole World Cup narrative about one player, and you could argue that didn't work out well.

France 98

That opening game was accompanied by trouble on the streets outside the stadium in Marseille, which may have coincided with the arrival of a double decker bus sponsored by *The Sun*, playing the national anthem and handing out bowler hats. Scholes was the star of the actual game, curling in a late second in brilliant sunshine after Alan Shearer had opened the scoring with a header.

The squad's training base at La Baule felt like a prison camp, and boredom began to kick in. While playing cards one night the players came up with a way to enliven things – when doing interviews they would compete to see who could get the most song titles into interviews. Gareth Southgate thus described the camp as 'hardly Club Tropicana', and Alan Shearer burst into a great grin when he realised that he had accidentally said 'Against All Odds' in an interview.

After a long week off England stumbled to a last-minute defeat against Romania, Michael Owen coming off the bench to score, which meant that they needed to at least draw with Colombia to progress. Beckham added to Darren Anderton's opener with a cathartic free kick that cemented his place back in the side, and Michael Owen could have had a hat trick as England were dominant.

The last 16 game against Argentina was a bona fide classic. Diego Simeone, the villain of the piece, won an early penalty by dragging his leg into David Seaman, who knew he'd been suckered. Just a few minutes later Michael Owen burst between Nelson Vivas and Roberto Ayala at speed and went down to win an equalising penalty which Shearer converted.

Argentina were so terrified of Owen's pace and directness that they dropped deeper and deeper, and gave him the room to score the goal of his life. He flicked the ball into space on the run close to half way, ignored the challenge of Chamot, swerved away from Ayala, and then calmly rammed the ball diagonally into the top corner before Scholes could nick the chance off him. A great goal, one of the greatest, and he was only 18. What an era of glory suddenly opened up before our eyes, with the likes of Beckham and Owen to call upon and Hoddle in charge!

Argentina equalised before half time with a free kick trick

that really shouldn't have worked, indeed hadn't worked before, and wouldn't again.

Then in the second half Simeone flattened Beckham, and while the England man was on the floor pretended to give him a friendly pat so he could pull his hair. Beckham flicked out an irritated boot, making minimal contact, but Simeone flung himself to the ground, conning the referee for the second time, and Beckham was off.

For the remaining 75 minutes through extra time England were immense. Hoddle reorganised brilliantly, and Adams and Ince drove the team on. Argentina never looked like sneaking a winner, whereas England had a Campbell goal disallowed for a foul on the keeper by Shearer, and a blatant handball in the area by Chamot waved away by a referee who just didn't know how to make friends.

David Seaman saved one in the shoot-out, Ince and Batty missed, and England were out, and you'd have to say unluckily so. Beckham carried the can, hung in effigy from a lamppost, booed at away games the next season, and enduring headlines such as 'Ten Heroic Lions, One Stupid Boy'.

England began their next qualification campaign poorly, and the fact is the longer he was in charge the more blinking odd Hoddle came to appear. His World Cup diary stated that he had only made one mistake, and that was not taking Eileen Drewery to France with the squad.

It wasn't just that, though. Stories emerged about him instructing his staff to walk around the pitch before the Argentina game, anti-clockwise for positive energy (in the Southern hemisphere you go clockwise, apparently), and his strange ritual of touching each player just above the heart with the Hand of Hod in the dressing room before games.

Then in January 1999 Hoddle gave an interview with the intention of explaining the Eileen Drewery thing and his own faith as a born-again Christian. His comments included mention of a not particularly Christian belief that the disabled are being punished for sins in a former life, which made him sound like a bit of a nutjob.

The self-righteous knee-jerk furore was ferocious. Hoddle must have suspected his goose was cooked when Prime Minister Tony Blair popped up on morning television to condemn the remarks as insensitive and unpalatable, and sure enough he wasn't able to ride it out.

Nonetheless, if his views were sincerely held – and why on Earth would he have mentioned them if they were not – he was surely entitled to them, and to remove him from his post for reasons which had nothing to do with football smacked nastily of religious intolerance, if not persecution. It certainly added to the impression that England managers were only there to serve one purpose as far as the tabloids were concerned, and that was to be ousted.

Keegan

Kevin Keegan took the reins briefly, completing qualification for Euro 2000 via a play-off win over Scotland, and then coming home with only a 1-0 win over Germany to show for it. There was trouble in Charleroi as well, and the whole episode is probably best forgotten.

Keegan had had success as manager of Newcastle, managing to infuse his sides with something of his own unstoppable energy as a player. In the England job he just looked out of his depth. He would stand on the touchline with his arms folded, his smile a mixture of pride and bewilderment, and there was a strong sense that once a game was under way he relied entirely on his players to change anything that needed changing – he'd done his job by picking the team. Sometimes his facial expression seemed to say 'Look at me, eh? Best seat in the house!'

When he resigned after losing a home World Cup qualifier to Germany – the last game played at the old Wembley, on the 7th of October, 2000 – there was a definite feeling that we'd regressed, that we were back at square one again. So much for the golden generation.

On
The Champions!

When I first started watching football[1] the European club competitions seemed set in stone. There was the European Cup, competed for by the champions of each of the member countries of UEFA. This was the top one, the most prestigious bauble. It was a knockout affair, with each round taking place over two legs, home and away, and away goals counting double in the event of a draw on aggregate. Famously, Real Madrid had dominated it to begin with, while English clubs had been a bit snooty about it. Manchester United won it in 1968, ten years after the Munich air disaster that had happened as they returned from an away leg. Celtic had won it in 1967 with a team made up entirely of players from Glasgow.

Then there was the European Cup Winners' Cup, into which the winners of the cup competition of every member country of UEFA would enter. Some of the countries started up a cup competition just so they could qualify for it. It was the second-

---

1 Note to self: must find another way to start these chapters off.

most prestigious of the club tournaments, and if the cup winner also won the league – and thus gained entry to the European Cup – then the runner up could enter. West Ham had won it in 1965, the second part of Bobby Moore's cup hat trick, and also Spurs in 1963, Manchester City in 1970, Chelsea in 1971 and Rangers in 1972.

Thirdly there was the UEFA Cup. This had started life as the faintly odd Inter-Cities Fairs Cup in the 1950s, when only cities could enter it and it took three years to finish. The first runners-up were London, who fielded a team made up of players from Spurs, Chelsea, Arsenal, West Ham, Crystal Palace, Brentford, QPR, Charlton, Orient, Millwall and Fulham. They lost the second leg 6-0 to Barcelona, perhaps because they didn't really know each other all that well.

This tournament morphed into the UEFA Cup in 1972, when Spurs beat Wolves in the final. Each member country got to enter three teams, the ones who finished second, third and fourth in the league, unless they'd won the cup, in which case skip them and carry on down.

And this is how things were until the tinkering began.

It was caused, as many things are, by a heady mixture of fear and greed. There had always been talk about the top clubs in Europe getting together and forming some sort of a super-league, and UEFA were worried that they might not be able to head that off, or be invited to be in charge of it. And then there was the arrival of satellite television as a big new player in television rights. They'd seen how much Murdoch had paid for the Premier League, and that was just one country. Imagine the deals they could do if they could pull off a similar revamp of their club competitions.

The problem for them was that all three of the tournaments

were knockout cup competitions, and so there was a danger that the top clubs, the ones from the big television markets such as Spain, France, Italy, Germany and the UK, could get knocked out early doors, perhaps by some upstart team from Poland or something, and that would take the edge off somewhat.

What they needed was something that wasn't altogether a league, but also wasn't a cup. Something that guaranteed the participants a minimum number of nice box office ties against each other, with hardly anyone getting knocked out until the very end.

So in 1992-93 they converted the European Cup to the UEFA Champions League. There would be knockout rounds to begin with, but then two groups of four, like in the World Cup, with the winners meeting in the final.

They commissioned branding and an anthem, which is an adaptation of Handel's *Zadok the Priest* and which culminates in the great choral blast of 'The Champions!', as the brass section continues twiddling on upwards behind, and they went about flogging the television rights to the whole kit and caboodle.

More tinkering in the next few seasons introduced knockout semi-finals after the groups, then knockout quarter-finals too, but essentially they were fine tuning. In 1997-98 UEFA decided to allow the runners- up in top European leagues to enter, thus undermining its own rebranding. They stopped short of rerecording the anthem – 'The Champions! And Runners-up!' The rather brutal thinking was that the quality of its premier tournament would be improved by including more top teams rather than having to play against the minnows from the smaller countries who didn't have access to such juicy television deals.

In 1999 Alex Ferguson's Manchester United made their way through the changing labyrinth, memorably beating Juventus in the semi-final, and came up against Bayern Munich in the final in Barcelona. They had already completed a domestic double, but suspensions were going to rob them of both Paul Scholes and Roy Keane, their two most influential players.

It seemed like it was trundling towards a dull and disappointing conclusion. Bayern took an early lead with a Mario Basler free kick in the sixth minute, and then held on comfortably with United barely threatening. Ferguson threw on Ole Gunnar Solskjaer and Teddy Sheringham in the last few minutes, and United started to create chances, but as the game went into injury time Bayern were still ahead. George Best left his seat to go and get into position for the trophy presentation.

Peter Schmeichel went up for a late corner, which sailed over his head. Ryan Giggs snapped in a tame shot, which Sheringham was able to turn in. Thirty seconds after the kick off, David Beckham swung in another corner, Sheringham nodded it down, and Solskjaer poked it in. As Ferguson memorably said in his post-match interview: 'Football, bloody hell!'

The following season there was a massive reboot. Now the top three leagues according to UEFA's mysterious coefficients, which is to say Spain, Italy and Germany, would get four teams in the competition. The next three leagues – England, France and the Netherlands – got to have three each.

Now there were eight groups who played their games before Christmas, and then the winners and runners up went into four more groups in the Spring. It was interminable.

UEFA also considered expanding the Cup Winners' Cup, from 32 to 64 teams, allowing two teams from each country, but they hadn't really thought that one through. What would the criteria for the second team be? Maybe they'd have to count back to losing semi-finalists, or even losing quarter-finalists, to get to clubs that weren't already in the new and bloated Champions League. In the end they merged the whole thing with the UEFA Cup and had done with it.

For four years UEFA persisted with a format in which it could take eighteen games for a team to get knocked out without even making the quarter-finals. They loved the television coverage they were getting and the many rights deals they had negotiated, but people were starting to grumble about the number of dead fixtures, and the sheer bloody relentlessness of it all. Not to mention the number of times they'd heard that anthem.

From 2003 onwards there was just one group phase before Christmas, and then a 16 team knockout in the Spring. It was still a bloated nonsense that thought far too highly of itself, but the reduction in games, though slight, seemed to suit the English participants.

In 2005 Liverpool reached the final against AC Milan. By half time it was game over, with Milan 3-0 up. It was my young son's birthday so we'd all gone out to the pictures, and I watched the game on video later on. At half time I started forward winding, thinking I might as well head for bed, when suddenly... what? What the hell?!

Steven Gerrard, Vladimir Smicer and Xabi Alonso made it three-all in six crazy second-half minutes, and the final went to a penalty shoot-out. Jerzy Dudek was the hero, copying Bruce Grobbelaar's spaghetti-legs routine from 1984 and saving from Andrea Pirlo and Andriy Shevchenko.

Arsenal reached the final in 2006, losing to Barcelona, and Liverpool lost their rematch with AC Milan in the 2007 final. Manchester United beat Chelsea on penalties in 2008 to win the trophy for a third time, and lost in the 2009 final. By this time England's performance was such – the Premier League had provided three semi-finalists three years running – that we were able to enter four teams each year, and such was the financial incentive to sit at Europe's top table that fourth place in the Premier League became like a trophy in itself.

In 2009 the UEFA Cup was rebooted as the Europa League, absorbing the frankly baffling Inter-Toto Cup along the way. With its qualification rounds starting absurdly early in the summer, and its unwieldy group format, and its many Thursday night games disrupting a team's league season, it has become a slightly awkward thing to find yourself involved in. A club like Burnley in 2018 can qualify with a seventh place finish that they could rightly be proud of, but the prize is to have your fixture list clogged up with an adventure that could take you months and months of travel and effort to get clear of.

The teams that finish third in the Champions League groups end up funnelling into the Europa League, so it really is quite hard to get eliminated from Europe altogether once you're in it. Chelsea did this very thing after an undistinguished defence of the Champions League, which they won in 2012 with a penalty shoot-out triumph over Bayern Munich, and ended up winning the Europa League in 2013.

Apart from that it's been a tricky one for English clubs to win. Liverpool did it in 2001, and Manchester United in 2017, while Fulham and Middlesbrough have made it to finals.

I can't say I care much about the European competitions any more. It's irritating that fourth place is an achievement that is supposed to count as a great success, because that success is measured only by money and continued exposure to an international audience that might buy your merchandise. Meanwhile Celtic, the first British winners of the old European Cup and the actual bona fide runaway champions of Scotland, have to wade through qualifying games (or not) against the similarly television-money-challenged AEK Athens to have even the sniff of a chance of sitting at the top table.

As for the Europa League: it takes a particular kind of administrative gormlessness to invent a competition that no one wants to enter let alone win, that takes the equivalent of an extra half a league season to reach the end of, and that is played on a Thursday, hitherto the only actual non-football day left to us by Rupert Murdoch.

On
The Golden Generation #2

Jeff Powell of the *Daily Mail* described it as selling 'our birthright down the fjord to a nation of seven million skiers and hammer-throwers who spend half their year living in total darkness'.

The Sun fulminated thus: 'What a climbdown. What a humiliation. What a terrible, pathetic, self-inflicted indictment.'

This was the welcome that greeted England's first non-English manager, a blast of charmless kneejerk xenophobia.

The tabloids missed quotable Cockney Terry Venables, but the F.A.'s new man Adam Crozier was being advised by David Dein, who'd broken new ground with his capture of Arsene Wenger and was open to the idea of a foreigner managing England – as long as it wasn't Arsene Wenger.

Caretaker Howard Wilkinson rather ruined his chances by saying that England, bottom of Group Nine, should give up on qualifying for the 2002 World Cup and concentrate on 2006, but that was the size of the shambles that Sven Goran Eriksson inherited.

His first game in charge was an encouraging 3-0 friendly win over Spain at Villa Park, where the photographers crowded in front of him to try and catch him out not knowing the words of the national anthem.

Qualifying wins against Finland, Albania and Greece revived England's campaign and began to turn the tide of opinion in his favour. Then came the away game in Germany, the return fixture of the game at Wembley that had ended with Keegan resigning in the toilet.

You could hardly have asked for a more English formation than the one favoured by our first foreign manager. Seaman in goal, Gary Neville, Cole, Ferdinand and Campbell as a back four, Gerrard, Scholes, Beckham and Barmby as a midfield four, and a big-man-little-man forward pairing of Heskey and Owen. And it worked, boy did it work.

England took Germany apart that evening, winning 5-1 even after giving them a goal start. Owen grabbed a hat trick, Gerrard and Heskey scored the others.

From then on the criticism faded away, and Sven was greeted as the new Messiah. Beckham's last minute free kick against Greece clinched qualification top of the group, and we were on our way to Japan.

Japan and South Korea 2002

With the sort of grim inevitability that persuades you that FIFA fixed the draw, England were scheduled to open their campaign in Japan against Sweden, the manager's hammer-throwing homeland.

The build-up was dominated by speculation about David Beckham's metatarsal, which was broken in a tackle by Argentinian hatchet man Aldo Duscher of Deportivo la

Coruna. The fact that England were due to play a grudge re-match against Argentina – of course they were – once they got to Japan only added spice to the speculation that he had been nobbled.

The English public knew more about metatarsal bones, and protective boots, and oxygen tent treatment than anyone really needed to (unless they were a doctor specialising in this particular injury, but most of those were busy giving interviews to the frantic press). There was also great anxiety among the Japanese public, who treated Beckham like a pop star, as well as amongst his many corporate sponsors hoping for great exposure during the Cup – the likes of Adidas, Pepsi, Brylcreem, Rage Software and Police sunglasses. Apparently.

In the event Beckham was fit enough to play in the opener, which was memorable for the thousands of flash bulbs going off every time the great man took a corner, and the giant cut-outs of Sven bouncing up and down in the area occupied by Swedish fans. It was a 1-1 draw, as these games always seem to be, with Sol Campbell heading England's goal.

The second game against Argentina was in the Sapporo Dome, an indoor venue, and the acoustics closely ressembled those of a large school hall. There was only one goal, and Beckham scored it, slamming a penalty – won by Michael Owen going over the leg of Mauricio Pochettino – straight down the middle. It was a great moment of redemption for the England captain, made all the sweeter because Diego Simeone was there to see it.

A scorching 0-0 draw with Nigeria and a comfortable 3-0 knockout of Denmark followed, as belief began to grow that this team, and this manager, might be the one to break through. The Golden Generation was missing Steven Gerrard, but Nicky Butt was named by Pelé as his player of the tournament – although it seems possible that he might have seen Paul Scholes and Butt playing together and thought 'That little ginger lad's everywhere, isn't he?!'

The quarter-final against a powerful Brazil side was played at Shizuoka, and it was another sizzlingly hot afternoon. Michael Owen put England in front midway through the first half, and England were looking good. Then just before half time Beckham jumped over a sliding tackle thinking the ball was going out of play, trying to protect his mending metatarsal. The slide kept the ball in, though, and England were caught out, Rivaldo applying the finish. 1-1 at the break.

Five minutes into the second half Ronaldinho took a free kick from a long way out, wide on the right. I was there, and you won't persuade me that he meant what he did. I saw the Brazilian forwards gesticulating with disgust as the cross sailed miles over their heads and out of play, only to suddenly run out of steam and drop over the helpless Seaman's head. The 'Floating Leaf', Ronaldinho tried to claim it was called. Fluking Lucky, more like.

Ronaldinho celebrated with a chicken dance round the running track, and then was sent off a few minutes later with exactly the same smile on his toothy face. England huffed and puffed but couldn't break them down. They needed a spark of invention, and Joe Cole was sat on the bench, but that is where he stayed as Sven brought on Kieron Dyer instead, then Darius Vassell and Teddy Sheringham. And then it was over.

Brazil won the tournament, beating the Germans 2-0 in the final, with Original Ronaldo gaining his own measure of redemption for 1998 by slotting both.

Euro 2004

Sven's England qualified for the 2004 Euros in Portugal with few alarms, and the Golden Generation was joined by the exciting youngster Wayne Rooney of Everton. It was his direct run that won England a penalty in the first game against France, but Fabien Barthez saved Beckham's effort. England were already a goal up, Frank Lampard having headed in a Beckham free kick in the first half. The game went into injury time, and then Zinedine Zidane curled a free kick past David James. Even as England absorbed the disappointment of conceding such a late equaliser, James brought down Thierry Henry and Zidane scored an even later winner from the spot.

After that setback, though, it was Rooney's show. He scored a couple against Switzerland in a 3-0 win, and then terrorised Croatia with his pace and power, notching a couple more as England won 4-2.

The quarter-final against the hosts began brilliantly, with a Michael Owen improvised finish on three minutes. It was downhill from there, though. Wayne Rooney's foot was broken by an unpunished stamp from Jorge Andrade, then Helder Postiga equalised with just seven minutes to go. In extra time Rui Costa and Frank Lampard scored to take the game to penalties.

Beckham missed the first, looking suspiciously at the turf. Rui Costa then missed for Portugal, before Ricardo took the headlines, the keeper saving from Darius Vassell then stepping up to strike the winning kick himself.

It had been another promising yet ultimately disappointing tournament for England. Rooney's injury was probably crucial, as he could have caused havoc as Portugal tired. The Golden Generation was otherwise all present and correct, with a stellar midfield of Gerrard, Lampard, Scholes and Beckham. So what was the missing ingredient? Just a bit of luck?

Greece showed just what could be achieved by a rather more ordinary generation, beating France, the Czech Republic and Portugal, all by 1-0, to lift the pot in front of a dismayed home crowd and a no doubt tearful Cristiano Ronaldo.

Germany 2006

Six weeks before England's opening group game against Paraguay the nation was plunged into another Metatarsal Watch. Out came the big protective boot and the oxygen tent once more, and this time it was star striker Wayne Rooney who had cracked a bone in a clash with Paolo Ferreira (of Portugal – I'm just saying). Like Beckham four years before, he somehow contrived to do this with the exact amount of time to spare that it was supposed to take for these things to heal, no more, no less.

That injury worry aside, however, you had only to look at the players numbered one to twelve in England's squad to see that surely this was the time for the Golden Generation to step up and actually win the thing. Paul Robinson, Gary Neville, Ashley Cole, Steven Gerrard, Rio Ferdinand, John Terry, David Beckham, Frank Lampard, Wayne Rooney, Michael Owen, Joe Cole and Sol Campbell had 594 caps between them, and averaged 49.5 apiece.

An early own goal squeaked them past Paraguay, and they took 83 minutes to open the scoring against Trinidad and Tobago, which rather sucked the air out of the optimism. Then they met Sven's Sweden again – see, I told you it was all sewn up – and went ahead through a quite brilliant Joe Cole volleyed goal. Marcus Allback equalised, and then Steven Gerrard grabbed a late second, only for Henrik Larsson – who would become the world's most dour imaginable pundit at Russia 2018 – to pop in an even later second equaliser.

Through to the last 16, England struggled in the heat against Ecuador, but sneaked through thanks to a trademark Beckham free kick from 30 yards out. The not-quite-fit Rooney played on his own up-front after a nasty knee injury to Michael Owen in the Sweden game. Incredibly, they now found themselves facing Luis Felipe Scolari for the third major quarter-final in a row, and he truly turned out to be Sven's nemesis. With the match still goalless after an hour, lone striker Rooney was challenged by two Portuguese defenders for the umpteenth time, and contrived to seemingly tread on Ricardo Carvalho's testicles. He maintained afterwards that it had been an accident, but the Portuguese players angrily surrounded the referee, and after Rooney was given a red card Cristiano Ronaldo was caught on camera winking at a colleague to confirm his belief that they had talked the ref into this.

Owen Hargreaves was brilliant after that, putting out fires all over the pitch, and England defended stoutly, but their only hope really was penalties, and that was no hope at all to this group of players. Ricardo was again the hero, saving from Lampard, Carragher and Gerrard, with only man-of-the-match Hargreaves scoring. And three of the Portuguese players, of course, including Ronaldo, the winker, whose kick was decisive.

The Cup was won on penalties by Italy – who were also supposed to be bad at them, by the way – after a draw principally memorable for Zinedine Zidane's headbutt on Marco Materazzi, after which he was obliged to leave the field early and walk right past the trophy on its little podium.

So what was it with Sven and the Golden Generation? Were they just unlucky? Or were they not really all that good?

In that quarter-final against Portugal they defended for their lives once they were down to ten men, but for the first hour they had already been playing like underdogs. They only had four shots in the whole game, the most important game of many of their lives, one which could have made their careers.

Did they freeze under the weight of expectation? They looked as strong a squad as England had ever put out, and yet were not convincing in any of their games. They defended well against Portugal when they were up against it, and they had a decent game against Sweden, but they seemed to be capable of so much better.

How about Sven himself? Gareth Southgate said that at half time against Brazil in Shizuoka in 2002 England had 'needed Churchill but got Iain Duncan Smith', which is pretty withering. Though what difference the cheerful insurance dog would have made is difficult to quantify precisely.

On
Total Nonsense

In 2004 the Football League clubs were getting more and more anxious about the gulf opening up between the Premiership and the rest. In every aspect – financial muscle, profile, attendances – the top flight had a seemingly insuperable advantage. What could be done, apart from to aspire to leave the Football League and join in?

Not to worry. Brian Mawhinney, the Tory grandee who had taken over as chairman of the Football League, had the answer. Division One, which used to be Division Two, would become the Championship. Division Two, which used to be Division Three, would become League One. And Division Three, which used to be Division Four, would become League Two. And if that didn't fix it, Brian Mawhinney didn't know what would.

Of course it is a total nonsense, a terminological cock up that has mangled football history backwards and forwards from that point. You can't say that a team won the championship any more, even if they are the undisputed champions of the land, because the Championship is now the second division, which used to be Division One.

It has led to the introduction of a whole new lexicon of phrases so that commentators, pundits and fans alike can make themselves understood. We were already dealing with 'top flight' and 'the top tier' to try and keep our football history connected to the pre-Premier League era, but more and more there were Premiership records and there were top-flight records, and you could feel patience with the notion that there had even been football before 1992 wearing thin.

The Championship, as it now was, would be referred to as 'the second tier', in order to avoid having to deal with the notion of competing for the championship of the Championship, rather than the actual championship of the country, which was the championship of the Premiership, which used to be Division One. League One and League Two you would have to refer to as the 'third or fourth level', or the 'third or fourth tier', or sometimes the old 'Third or Fourth Division', just to keep it straight in people's heads that there hadn't actually been a mass promotion, even though it sounded like there had.

Then there was the anxiety that this all sounded like the prelude to a second tier breakaway, which is to say a Championship breakaway, which would create a new gulf perhaps as large as that which currently existed below the Premiership between what used to be Divisions Two and Three, but which was now the Championship and League One. And what would that new breakaway division be called? Premiership 2 was mooted for a time, and what would that have meant? League One, the third tier, becoming the Championship now? League Two, which was Division Four, becoming Division One?

Did this rebranding make an iota of difference to anything

apart from the verbal diarrhoea it generated? Did it bring a single extra fan through the turnstiles, raise a single extra pound for any of the Football League clubs?

Of course it didn't. It was then and remains now, like so many of the things Brian Mawhinney had to do as Tory party chairman, pointless and stupid.

On
Wembley Stadium

The Twin Towers. The hallowed turf. The white horse cup final. Geoff Hurst hits the bar. Some people are on the pitch, they think it's all over… it is now!

It is all over now, of course, because the grand old stadium, the first place I ever saw a five quid burger, was pulled down at the start(ish) of the new millennium and replaced by something much brighter, newer and way more expensive than it was supposed to be.

After seeing the smashing new stadia for the 1998 World Cup suddenly good old Wembley, which had been absolutely fine for Euro 96, was feeling a bit shabby and past it. The powers-that-be didn't want to wait for England to be awarded another World Cup – I mean, how long could that take? – still counting – they wanted a new one and they wanted it now.

And that wasn't all. France had won the World Cup and then the Euros and were the dominant force in world football. People were wondering how they did that, and put it down to their much-admired centralised national youth academy at Clairefontaine, which seemed to be churning out mightily impressive young technicians like a veritable production line.

So the F.A. decided they wanted one of them as well.

They had already been milking the old place, having controversially decreed that FA Cup semi-finals would be played there as well as the final, even when, as in 1994 for example, Manchester United were playing Oldham Athletic, or when it was Sheffield United against Sheffield Wednesday, as it had been the previous year.

It put some noses out of joint, hauling thousands of fans down to London, especially when television decided to make one of the semis on a Sunday, which was not so easy for train travel.

And it did dilute the magic of Wembley as a dream for football fans, especially when they started playing the play-off finals there and half the teams in the country got a go.

While the new one was built, they moved the Cup final to Cardiff, and played international games all over the place – Old Trafford, Villa Park, Elland Road, the Etihad, Leicester, Middlesbrough, Ipswich – all of which was tremendously popular and provided some stirring atmospheres. Ironically the F.A. could hardly have demonstrated more clearly how little the new Wembley was needed.

They were committed now, though, and as costs went up and up over £700 million, the project drained all the money out of the St George's Park initiative, which was supposed to provide the next generation of players to grace the hallowed turf. Actually, among the many problems encountered was the fact that the original turf was insufficiently hallowed and had to be dug up.

When it was finally ready, with its new trademark arch rather than its former trademark twin towers – the arch is structural by the way and holds the whole thing up – the F.A. immediately started packing as many games in there as they could, to try and recoup some of the runaway costs.

The place somehow never looks full, on account of the fact that the blocks immediately opposite the television camera position are only intermittently occupied by the prawn sandwich brigade. At time of writing Spurs are using the place for home games while they wait for clearance to use the newly-rebuilt White Hart Lane, and the FA are in talks with Shahid Khan, the owner of the Jacksonville Jaguars American (not really football) football team, about taking the whole thing off their hands for 900 million quid.

New stadia

Delays and overspend have become familiar aspects of the modern game, as more and more clubs have felt the need to build new stadia. Before that, of course, there are usually months of stories about planning permission, and complaints from locals at whatever new site is being contemplated at the thought of hooligans urinating in their front gardens or something.

Tottenham are the latest to have to put back their opening fixture because of unforeseen factors, and they played in the new Wembley all of last season, demonstrating that they were actually capable of filling an ambitious new ground, which must have been a relief.

To my way of thinking, football clubs surrender decades of history and their iconic homes very easily. Maybe my view is coloured by the fact that my attempt to complete the full set and join the 92 Club – if such a thing even still exists – has been perennially thwarted by the construction of more and more identikit concrete and plastic bowls. Comfortable? Certainly. On the other side of the ring road nowhere near a railway station? Probably. But I've been hovering around the 82 mark for years, despite the fact that I have actually seen Oldham play on more than 130 grounds in my (considerable) time. Give me a break, why don't you?

West Ham is one I have now to re-visit, since they occupied the new Olympic Stadium as an inexplicable gift from the taxpayer. Upton Park, their historic old stadium, was offered up to the makers of the upcoming film *Final Score* so they could blow it up. It was one final heart-breaking indignity for Hammers fans to suffer, seeing their beloved home destroyed on celluloid by Pete Bronson, the bloke who was Bond, and the other feller, the one who talks about his monster turds in *Guardians of the Galaxy*.

sports direct dot com Park

Not every club can put together the exorbitant sums needed for a whole new ground, of course. Oldham just about managed a new stand by hook or by crook, after playing at a three-sided ground for several seasons. They also managed to flog off part of their iconic history along the way, joining the mammon-sullied band who have allowed sponsors to rename their very home grounds. And these names can change over and over again, a couple of seasons at a time, with the club's very identity ruinously eroded.

Oldham Athletic did a deal with Mike Ashley to sponsor Boundary Park. Part of the deal involved Sports Direct putting a club shop in the new stand that was being built so that the club didn't have to run one, which was a bit of a shame. I always liked it when the club shop was called Latique – little bit of a pun there, always welcome. The ground, Oldham's home for more than a century, became known as sportsdirect.com Park. All little letters (apart from the P in Park). The rationale for this was that whenever the name appeared in a match report or an article on the internet, the new ground name would automatically be underlined by internet magic and provide a hyperlink to the Sports Direct website, in the most brutally insensitive and cynical piece of sponsorship I have yet heard of.

Of course nobody used the new name, because it was just stupid. Also it just didn't fit the rhythm of the taunting chant aimed at home supporters at away games – 'where were you at sportsdirect dot com Park?' Roy Butterworth, the old chap who does the match commentary on the Latics website, dutifully tried to correct himself whenever he said Boundary Park by accident, which was every couple of minutes, and in the end the whole thing was quietly dropped and never ever mentioned again.

On
Murdoch Marches Onward

Rupert Murdoch's death grip on football continued into the new millennium. His new three-year deal in 2004 took the number of games he was showing per season up from 110 to 138, and the rise of Sky went hand in hand with the flourishing of the Premiership. He'd even managed to get more matches for marginally less money in this new deal, as he only paid a (still eye-watering) £1.024 billion for the seasons 2004-05 to 2006-07, where previously he had been forking out £1.2 billion.

Had we reached the tipping point? Were we getting to a place where the Premiership needed Sky even more than Sky needed the Premiership? Would Rupert soon be calling the tune even more than he already did?

The sense that Sky was the only player in the big game was heightened by the ITV Digital fiasco. Rather than compete with Murdoch for the top flight, the new company (previously ONDigital) did a lucrative deal with the rump of the Football League for lower division games. Sky had been part of setting this outfit up, originally, with Carlton and Granada, but had been obliged to leave because of competition and monopoly rules, and so this television deal was in opposition to Sky's seeming mastery. The Football League clubs were delighted – finally they were going to see some of the television rights bonanza for themselves, rather than being handed some token crumbs by the cartel of the Greedy League.

Unfortunately, however, ITV Digital went bust, and the Football League's windfall went with it. A couple of clubs had already spent the money they were expecting to get and found themselves in serious financial strife. Bradford City, for instance, which went into receivership with debts of £36 million.

So Murdoch was still laughing, showing live Premiership games on Saturday lunchtime, tea time, Sunday afternoons, Monday evenings. He was still forbidden from showing live coverage at 3.00 on a Saturday, due to an archaic regulation that had been put in place to protect attendances at that time. Sky's response was to establish another way of enslaving the viewer.

Soccer Saturday, presented by the estimable force of broadcasting nature that is Jeff Stelling, offered up the videprinter, descendant of the teleprinter that used to tap out the final scores as they came in of a Saturday teatime before the wrestling came on. Now, though, it was there from the kick off, showing every goal, every sending off, every half time and full time. And in the meantime we were getting updates from a panel of old pros who *were* allowed to watch games on television at 3.00 on a Saturday, telling us what they had just seen happen as we watched them seeing it.

It was oddly compelling, certainly better than watching the scores coming in on Teletext, which was the old way of keeping in touch with things if you weren't going to a game. To be honest, it's been going so long, and has been slavishly imitated by both the BBC and BT, that it is beginning to show its age. The old pros are no longer quite so in touch with the players – in particular how to pronounce their foreign surnames – and in return the viewers can barely remember them in their playing days. *Soccer AM*, the laddish morning magazine show, has also seen better days. Indeed, it's never been the same since Tim Lovejoy left, and even he always managed to give the impression that he'd rather be doing a music show.

In 2006, though, things took a bit of a turn for Rupert. The European Commission insisted that exclusive rights should not be sold to just one company, and suddenly Setanta Sports, an Irish company, had acquired the rights to two of the six packages on offer, pinching 42 of Murdoch's matches. What's more, between Sky and Setanta, the total paid shot up to £1.7 billion, which was another huge bonanza for the top clubs.

Setanta had over-reached, of course, and went bust in 2009, when their packages were picked up by ESPN, which showed games from 2009-2013. Since then, Sky has been sharing the marketplace with BT Sports, and from 2019-20 onwards there will be 20 live matches a season on Amazon.

The first deal after the Setanta collapse remained at roughly the same level, but since then it has skyrocketed again, to more than £3 billion for 2013-16, and then well over £5 billion for 2016-19. They are paying something like £11 million per match, and you have to wonder whether that is a sustainable model, don't you? Some of these games are only watched by a few hundred thousand people, while on other channels high-class dramas that cost considerably less are expected to rack up way better ratings than that or face the consequences.

But so much money coming into the game – that's got to be good for everyone, right?

The Premier League was anxious to announce that £56 million – i.e. about one percent – would be set aside for grassroots projects, including 50 artificial pitches. Although here's a thing: if you're going to earmark money for artificial pitches, maybe you should come up with a different term than 'grassroots projects' to describe your extravagant generosity.

How the money gets split up

Bearing in mind that the Sky and BT deal is not the only income the Premier League clubs get to share amongst themselves – there are overseas television rights, too, and various commercial sponsorships – here is how the clubs split last season's £2.475 billion amongst themselves.

First of all there is an equal share out of a large proportion of the television money, amounting to £82 million per club. So far so egalitarian.

Then there are facilities fees relating to how many times a club gets to appear in live matches. In 2017-18 the top earners were Manchester United (who finished second) and Liverpool (fourth) who both pocketed an extra £33.9 million. At the bottom end of this sliding scale were relegated Swansea and Stoke, struggling Huddersfield and Watford, and resolutely unglamorous Europa League qualifiers Burnley, who each drew down an additional £12.5 million.

And then, because the object of the exercise is to arrange the clubs in order of wealth, give or take a position or two, there is 'merit money' to consider. Manchester City won £39.8 million for taking top spot, with the prize diminishing by roughly £2 million a place down to bottom club West Brom, who were awarded just the £2 million.

All of which adds up, and how. Manchester United did the

best out of all that with a winning score of £153.7 million, while even the three relegated clubs made somewhere in the region of £100 million apiece. That is before you even start thinking about attendance money and merchandising, areas where Manchester United in particular also have a big wedge to add on. Another £112 million in match day income, for example, £75 million from Adidas for the kit deal, and a whopping £276 million in other commercial income. Wages accounted for 45 percent of their enormous £581 million turnover in 2016-17, and they still needed the £77.5 million prize money for winning the Europa League to put them £57 million into overall profit.

That is the size and speed of the gravy train that Murdoch turned English football into, so it's small wonder that clubs get desperate about being thrown off it.

This huge guaranteed income even for finishing in the bottom three is why the Championship play-off is now habitually described as 'the richest game in football'. The winner can expect to pick up £100 million just for being in the Premier League for a season.

Such is the reliance on television money for the Premier League clubs that half of them (according to 2016-17 figures) could still make a profit without any matchday ticket receipts at all. Bournemouth have the smallest ground capacity in the Premier League (although they plan a bigger stadium, obviously). Staggeringly, match ticket receipts only account for something like 4 percent of their income, with 91 percent coming from the television share-out, and the rest from various other activities.

It's not hard to see why priorities have changed at the top. Lower down the leagues, of course, matchday revenue is far more significant as a proportion of the whole. In the Premier

League, however, when Liverpool supporters hold up banners protesting at the sixty quid away ticket price at the Emirates which read 'Football without fans is nothing', actually the clubs are pretty much shrugging and saying 'You know what? We'd manage.'

But... don't they need you as much as you need your fix? Because suppose there were no fans, or let's say significantly fewer, that would start to impact upon the attractiveness of the product that the clubs are flogging, wouldn't it? If the stadia were cavernous and echoing, and you could hear blokes farting and mumbling to themselves? So one might think it'd be broadly in the clubs' interests to bring prices right down, but are they doing that? Are they crackers.

Parachute payments

Of course, when such huge amounts of cash are involved just for participating, it is going to hurt when you get booted out of nirvana onto your backside.

This is why the Premiership/Premier League clubs voted themselves what are called parachute payments, a unique phenomenon in world sport.

When relegated, a Premier League club will continue to receive a proportion of the fees that were theirs in their last season in the top tier. In the first season it is 55 percent, in the second 45 percent, and in the third it falls to 20 percent. After that they are on their own, but if they haven't managed to translate this massive financial advantage into promotion then frankly no one is going to have a very great deal of sympathy for them.

These parachute payments, this compensation for failure,

hugely distorts the playing field in the Championship. Indeed, when a team goes straight through the next trapdoor and drops into League One, as Sunderland have done, it is extremely galling for the shoestring operations they will find themselves facing in their massive Stadium of Light to know that they will still have £25 million to play with, just for failing to stay in the Premier League. And if they don't manage to make it straight back up to the Championship they will still receive a bonus of £11 million to fund a second go.

It's true that relegated teams generally find themselves saddled with huge contracts for the players they signed in a desperate last ditch attempt to turn things around, but rather than compensating them for this epic mismanagement perhaps the Premier League should consider insisting on relegation clauses in player contracts that would reduce the wage bill and make these absurdly unfair parachute payments unnecessary.

Football economics are not like real economics. They are insane. In 2016-17 fourteen of the Championship clubs spent more than 100 percent of their turnover (how do you even do that?) on staff costs – i.e. the wages of players and management, because they're not paying the turnstile guy or the mascot more than minimum wage peanuts, if that. This is a desperate gamble, trying to get back aboard the Premier League gravy train. And of couse there isn't room for all of them.

The parachute payments look even more unfair when you consider the so-called 'solidarity payments' that the Premier League graciously vouchsafes out of the goodness of its collective black heart for the Football League clubs who have not yet been fortunate enough to hitch a ride on the main gravy train.

Each Championship club receives £4.3 million out of the

Premier League pot, but this doesn't help much in levelling things out with the clubs receiving parachute payments because they get this as well. League One clubs get a mere £645,000, while those in League 2 pick up £430,000.

These amounts are relatively pitiful, but even so they are vitally important for the continued existence of clubs at the bottom end, scraping along as they are.

It didn't have to be like this.

If – a big if – the Football League had had the balls to stand up to the Premier League breakaway in 1992. Or if the Football Association had not been so blindly eager to put one over on the Football League and instead acted for the benefit of the whole game, which is supposed to be its whole raison d'être. If, if, if…

Then the principle could have been established that the massive windfalls provided by Sky, BT and others were to be distributed all the way down the Football League. Not equally, of course, I don't believe that would ever have happened, but with enough for everyone to ensure the integrity of the competition as a whole, and make it possible for all the clubs to believe that they could still one day make it to the top table.

As it is, football has lost something essential thanks to Murdoch's intervention and the staggering mismanagement of it by the authorities. Now there is a top six that competes for the trophies and European places, and the rest of the Premier League competes to a greater or lesser extent just to stay in there receiving its largesse.

The Championship below has a top group that is funded by parachute payments, trying desperately to get back into the top flight before the money runs out, while at least half the division knows they cannot get any higher whatever they do. Below that, League One is usually distorted by the presence of one or two clubs that shouldn't really have dropped down there who will snag the promotion places, while smaller clubs who have a bright season, like Shrewsbury did last time, will ultimately fall away.

And the whole charmless business of football clubs shuffling into precisely the positions they would occupy if you arranged them all in order of wealth continues.

Where will all this lead?

The wholesale surrender of football's very soul to Sky seems to me to have changed something even more fundamental about the game, and that is its relationship to the youngest generation. And naturally that will determine – has already determined – its relation to the fans in the years and decades to come. It must seem like there can only be more expansion and boom ahead, mustn't it? But that is because football is run by people who only understand success in the simplest and most brutish of financial terms. What if the seeds of football's decay and boom have already been sown? What if they have built in their own obsolescence?

My own three sons have grown up in the era of live football every day. When I hear them and their friends talking it seems to be roughly akin to the way my friends and I would talk about players we admired, but more often than not it turns out that the attributes they are discussing are stats on Football Manager or FIFA.

All three of my boys are to an extent interested in football. They will come with me to an Oldham game, for a day out, but their enjoyment (or otherwise) is casual. They are entirely immune to the sort of all-consuming obsession that I developed at their ages. This may of course be because Oldham's last two decades haven't exactly been thrills and spills, but then they haven't felt drawn to anyone else either.

They got into the Russia World Cup, massively so, which was a huge part of my own enjoyment of that, being able to share it with the three of them – actually, my oldest boy was in South East Asia, and watched South Korea knock Germany out in a bar in Cambodia in the middle of the night with a South Korean travelling companion, an experience I am seriously jealous of. And my middle lad spent a week in Croatia during the tournament, also a memorable place to be.

So far, though, there are no signs that all this has fuelled a more lasting passion for the game as a whole, now that the Premier League has cranked back into 24/7 action. Not like Mexico '70 did for me, when I started hoovering up all the football I could get.

So what is it that is different for kids now? I think it is the very ubiquity of football that acts against them engaging with it to the same extent my generation did. It has become possible to follow it in a much more shallow and unemotional way, as it is possible to follow a soap opera by watching one episode a month. It may be on all the time, but that doesn't mean you have to consume all of what is available. It is actually off-putting that there is so much coverage; it makes it feel less important, not more. It feels disposable – there will always be another game along.

And what this means, it seems to me, is that football risks breeding a whole future generation of fans whose interest in its product could turn out to be similarly disposable.

What if they have allowed Rupert Murdoch to throttle the golden goose? Or, alternately, to have stuffed it so full that its over-delicious liver actually explodes and kills it?

On
The Brolly and
the Heavy Shirt

After whipping up a frenzy of Rooney-inspired enthusiasm, the media turned when England lost out at Euro 2004, and now began to call for the Swede's removal, rather than contenting itself with exposing his affair with Ulrika Jonsson off the telly and making jokes about the lifts in his shoes. The players threatened to go on strike, and the F.A. responded by extending the manager's contract up to Euro 2008.

In January 2006, however, Eriksson was duped by the *News of the World's* 'fake sheikh' into believing that he was being offered the Aston Villa job, and was taped claiming he could definitely get David Beckham to sign. It all seemed more than a little lame, but shortly after this it was announced that Eriksson would leave after the 2006 World Cup. Chalk another one up for the tabloids. After all, they know what the fans want: it's to build up our hopes to unreasonable levels while undermining our chances at every turn.

After Eriksson left, the F.A.'s first choice to succeed him was Luis Felipe Scolari, who had been responsible for knocking England out of the previous three tournaments. He turned the offer down, citing a fear of media intrusion into his life, but clearly rattled by the thought of the fake sheikh.

Mac the Knife

Steve McClaren had been a coach at Manchester United when they won the treble, and Sven's assistant at the time of the 5-1 in Munich and at the three subsequent major tournaments. On top of that, he was the most recent English manager to win any kind of trophy, the League Cup with Middlesbrough in 2004, so his credentials were pretty good. His reception was lukewarm, though, though he tried to drum up a bit of enthusiasm by bringing Terry Venables in as his assistant. He also acquired the services of PR guru Max Clifford, whose previous involvement in football had been to fabricate the story of Tory MP David Mellor having sex in a Chelsea shirt, which had loosened the nation's grip on its breakfast some years before.

McClaren began by dropping some senior players, including Sol Campbell, David James, and the 31 year-old previous captain David 'Goldenballs' Beckham, despite the latter vowing to fight to retain his place. This earned him the nickname 'Mac the Knife', which is a bit naff but a lot cooler than the nickname he ended up with.

After an OK start, the qualification campaign began to slip off the rails with a couple of 0-0 draws against Macedonia and Israel, and a damaging 0-2 defeat away in Croatia, which featured a frankly comical own goal by Gary Neville which skipped over Paul Robinson's boot as he attempted a routine clearance.

The stage was set for a messianic return for Beckham, and

he duly laid on goals for Crouch and Owen in a hope-reviving 3-0 win over Estonia. Duly inspired, England secured wins by the same scoreline against nearest rivals Russia and Israel even without Beckham, and came to the last game at home to already-qualified Croatia needing only a draw.

Surprisingly, McClaren left Beckham on the bench and replaced Robinson with Scott Carson, who let a shot squirm through his hands after eight minutes and was beaten again just a few minutes later. Beckham came on at half time and set up the equaliser for Crouch after Lampard had dragged England back into it from the spot, but Croatia weren't finished and Petric beat Carson from 25 yards to knock England out.

It was raining, of course, and McClaren took refuge under a huge F.A. red and blue umbrella, leading to the headline 'The Wally with the Brolly' and a new nickname. Of course, if he hadn't he'd have got soaking wet and they'd have only come up with something else. 'The Bloke who got Soaked', something like that.

McClaren had always seemed like a nice enough guy, eager to please – as he had shown with his endlessly amusing Dutchman-speaking-English accent while manager of Twente Enschede – but in way over his head. His walking out of a press conference after a couple of minutes, telling the assembled press to just write what they wanted to write, spoke of a man unable to handle a high-profile job. Still, he didn't have to do it for too long, as his time was up almost before he'd had time to dry out the brolly, and up till then it was the shortest time anyone had been in charge of England. Up till then…

The Taskmaster

The cash-register-chinned Italian Fabio Capello was a stellar appointment, having only recently managed Real Madrid. Some were disappointed that the new manager was not English, including Sepp Blatter, although what it had to do with him was not clear.

The fact that he had a reputation as a disciplinarian was greeted with enthusiasm, as though Eriksson and McClaren had somehow been too slack and easy-going and that had been the problem.

After nine wins out of ten in qualifying for South Africa, the F.A. swiftly removed a release clause in Capello's contract to fend off interest from Internazionale. Once the World Cup got under way they surely began to regret that.

Eriksson had created almost a holiday camp atmosphere in Baden Baden at the last World Cup, with controversy over the presence of the WAGs, the wives and/or girlfriends. Capello, by contrast, was accused of running a harsh and boring military-style camp at the Royal Bafokeng Sports Club in Bloemfontein, but he dismissed that afterwards as a 'loser's excuse'.

Capello's strict regime apparently caused friction with the players. And he was seriously disenchanted with them after the first two disappointing draws with the USA and Algeria. 'I don't understand why during a game we don't change the rhythm or the speed. We are really slow', he complained.

Rio Ferdinand, the captain, said that the manager brought in a prison-camp mentality and left the team devoid of tactics. 'We had expected ideas and creativity', he said. 'Instead, Capello's attitude was, "I'm the boss and you'll do what I say all day, every day. He seemed to need to show us how strong and disciplinarian he could be and was so aggressive sometimes it was just ridiculous."'

Rob Green, Capello's first-choice keeper – which is to say his first first-choice keeper – at the 2010 World Cup, spoke of the manager's lack of communication with players and the culture being one of fear. He claimed that the players were fat-shamed, constantly weighed and told they were overweight, even right before big games. He wasn't told he was playing until just before the Rustenburg game against the USA, in which he made a calamitous error, and afterwards Capello barely spoke to him, merely saying it was too big an error, and that he wouldn't be playing next time. According to Green the players lived in fear of making mistakes and being punished for them.

For his part, Capello believed that years without success weighed increasingly heavily on the team's shoulders, saying: 'This never-ending '66, the returning ghost, something with its white tentacles… and you can no longer perform in the way that you should.'

England scraped past Slovenia with a Jermaine Defoe poacher's goal, and then came up against Germany in the last-16. Again it was a tale of what might have been, as England quickly went two goals down. They fought back, though, and pulled one back through Matthew Upson. Then, in the most controversial moment of the tournament, they were denied an equaliser as Frank Lampard's shot cannoned down off the crossbar clearly over the line, but play was waved on. The referee and linesman were conned by Manuel Neuer, the German keeper, who grabbed the ball and played on as if nothing had happened. This incident is often cited as the one that led to the introduction of goal-line technology at World Cups. England conceded a couple of fast breakaway goals in the second half to make the scoreline a flattering 4-1 to Germany, but in truth they were quicker and more flexible than we were and deserved to win.

Capello's reputation had taken a battering, and the tension in the squad was clearly seen in Wayne Rooney's snarling reaction to being booed off the pitch after the draw with Algeria. The Italian kept his job into qualification for Euro 2012, but the honeymoon was well and truly over.

In the end there were a couple of off-field issues that really tripped Capello up. One was his promotion of something called The Capello Index, whereby he would provide his own player ratings for a newspaper, which never seemed like a good idea. The F.A. refused him permission to publish his ratings until after the World Cup, and then they appeared to be a mostly meaningless mish-mash, and to two decimal places.

The other was the on-off captaincy of John Terry. Terry had been named captain by McClaren in succession to David Beckham, and had captained all through the qualification games for 2010. Then, in February 2010, Capello removed the armband after allegations that Terry had had an affair with the former girlfriend of team mate Wayne Bridge, which led to a short-lived super-injunction. This was lifted partly because it became clear that everybody already knew about it, and there was fevered speculation as to whether the two would shake hands when their clubs played one another – they did not.

Terry was replaced as captain by Rio Ferdinand, but in South Africa it was Terry still who seemed to be acting as the team's spokesman, arranging a 'clear the air' meeting about tactics and agitating for Joe Cole's inclusion in the team. Capello said that Terry had made 'a very big mistake' in challenging his authority.

Nonetheless, in March 2011 Rio Ferdinand was injured, and Capello reinstated Terry as captain, only for Terry to become embroiled in another scandal, when he was charged with racially abusing Anton Ferdinand, Rio's brother. This time the

F.A. stripped Terry of the position, and Capello used this as a pretext to resign a job that by then he was clearly desperate to escape from.

On
Contact

Is there anything more depressing for the football fan of a certain vintage than hearing post-match discussions about 'contact'?

Oh, look, there was definite 'contact' there, if he feels that 'contact' he's entitled to go down.

Alan Shearer ought to be ashamed of himself. In his playing days he gave every impression of being a man who could only be nudged off the ball if the defender was driving a transit van. Now he finds himself on *Match of the Day* every week justifying penalty claims by seeking out microscopic whiffs of 'contact'.

Never mind that the 'contact' in question would barely be enough to spill a forward's cup of tea let alone send him sprawling face down in agony. 'Contact', that's the thing you're not allowed to have now, that's the curse that needs to be stamped out.

But wasn't football once a full-blooded 'contact' sport? Wasn't it once populated by hard men, with nicknames like 'Psycho', 'Chopper', and 'Bites Yer Legs'?

These once-fearsome worthies are now the subject of perennial wistful filler articles, usually headlined after a song by Peter, Paul and Mary, a notorious trio of hatchet men from the early 1960s.

Where Have All The Hard Men Gone?

Long time passing. Well, not passing exactly. Long time hoofing the ball into the fabled Row Z or out for a throw in off the winger's cracked shinpads.

The reducers have been reduced. Because now you can't tackle from behind, you can't slide, you can't leave the ground, you can't even raise your foot to challenge for a bouncing ball.

You can get a yellow card for kicking the ball away as an opponent is about to start lining up a free kick. You can get a yellow card for taking your shirt off after you have scored a goal, or for celebrating with the fans of your own team. You can get one for carrying on after being flagged offside and trying to pop the ball into the net – and, I'm sorry, but everyone in the ground wants to see this happen, either to fuel their sense of grievance or for the sheer *schadenfreude* of it all.

Who were all these changes for? Not the fans, surely. Don't we all, secretly, want to see challenges that make us do the face that Joaquin Phoenix does in *Gladiator* when watching the blood spurt skywards from a hard-but-fair Russell Crowe tackle?

When I first got into football every team had a hard man. Liverpool had Tommy Smith, who Bill Shankly said was not born, but quarried. Chelsea had Ron 'Chopper' Harris. Manchester United and England had gap-toothed enforcer Nobby Stiles. Leeds had Norman Hunter, of course, who took his cumbersome 'Bites Yer Legs' nickname from a banner in the crowd. Then Leeds also had Johnny Giles and Billy Bremner. And Jackie Charlton, with his famous little black book. And Joe 'Jaws' Jordan. And the rest of them were no pushovers, either.

Later there was Graeme Souness, and Kenny Burns, who once head-butted Arsenal's Richie Powling when they were waiting for a free kick to be taken, just to let him know he was there.

Hard nuts weren't confined to the English leagues, either. Italy's Claudio Gentile fouled Maradona 11 times in a 1982 World Cup game, and afterwards opined, 'Football is not for ballerinas.' Not then, it wasn't, anyway.

Later still there was the Crazy Gang, featuring *Gladiators* presenter John 'Fash the Bash' Fashanu, and Vinnie Jones, later Juggernaut off of the *X-Men*.

Stuart 'Psycho' Pearce was an England regular and sometime captain, as was Terry Butcher, back when it was possible to emerge from a brutal encounter bloodied but unbowed, in a shirt a different colour to the one the rest of your team were playing in. Now you have to go off for a clean shirt if you have a little nose bleed or a bit of a grazed eyebrow.

David Batty managed to get into a fist fight with his own team mate, Graeme le Saux, and it could be said that Batty and Paul 'The Guv'nor' Ince both confirmed their hard man status with their costly inability to hit something the shape and size of a barn door in the penalty shoot-out against Argentina.

Duncan Ferguson drew a 12-match ban and three months in chokey for head-butting Raith Rovers' John McStay, and that was in Scotland, where the head-butt has long been a casual greeting. In 2001 two burglars had the bright idea to rob the hard-man striker's house while he was in it. One got away, but Big Dunc put the other one in hospital.

And of course there was Roy Keane, who famously said of his deliberate assault on Alf-Inge Haaland: 'The ball was there (I think). Take that you cunt.'

It's been subtle, and has been happening for quite a while, but the way the game has gone it's hard to imagine any of these guys lasting 90 minutes on a regular basis now.

The 1970 F.A. Cup final between Chopper's Chelsea and Revie's Leeds was famously brutish. Staged on a pitch already churned up by the *Horse of the Year* Show, there were punches, head-butts, and meaty challenges galore. Ron Harris injured himself injuring Eddie Gray early on, while Norman Hunter made a strong case for a new nickname – 'Thumps Yer Head'. Now maybe the original referee was on the lenient side – Hugh McIlvanney wrote in *The Observer*: 'At times it appeared that Mr Jennings would give a free kick only on production of a death certificate' – but he only booked one player, Chelsea's Ian Hutchinson. In 1997 David Elleray, then a top referee, reviewed the game and reckoned that he would have dished out six red cards and twenty yellows. Some players he'd have sent off twice, apparently, although presumably the second time would have been for sneaking back onto the pitch after being sent off the first time. And that disgraceful catalogue of cards was by the standards of more than twenty years ago, remember. Nowadays there would surely not have been enough players on the field to complete the match.

The protection racket

So how did this happen? Money is at the bottom of it, naturally. This is football.

You could date the shift back to Arsene Wenger's arrival at Arsenal in 1996, and his avowed intention to play 'modern football'. The sub-text being that British football was a neanderthal backwater compared to the sophistication of continental Europe.

In fairness, his first Arsenal teams could mix it with anyone. Tony Adams, Nigel Winterburn and Steve Bould were decidedly tough nuts, Patrick Vieira went toe-to-toe with Roy Keane on a regular basis, while Martin Keown can often be heard discussing 'reducers' with a wistful chuckle during his commentary stints.

Wenger's influence began to spread, and it was reinforced by the success of tiki-taka in Spain. Possession football became all the rage, and the nature of the game began to shift away from blood and also thunder.

Fabulously wealthy owners started picking up our biggest clubs. Abramovich bought Chelsea, the Glazers somehow took over Manchester United by leveraged *leger-de-main*, and Sheikh Mansour transformed Manchester City.

The television rights bonanza skewed the game's money-to-sense ratio out of whack for ever, and naturally the world's finest attacking talents were eager to stick their noses in the trough. Enormous fees were being paid routinely, obscene wages being dished out – and those at the very top wanted their precious show-pony investments protected from an old-style clogging.

All of which means we have seen years of drip-drip-drip legislation designed to protect purveyors of silky skills over the destroyers that were once their natural nemesis.

If you listen to some post-match interviews these days you'd think it was still carnage out there. Recently Manchester City supremo Pep Guardiola whinged that his pricy prima donnas 'need more protection' after a supposed horror tackle on wing-er Leroy Sane that ended up keeping him out of action for all of

three weeks. Opposing old-school manager Neil Warnock's re-
tort that Pep was 'in England now' was undermined somewhat
by the fact that he was speaking in Cardiff, and more by the
fact that the hard-as-nails English football that Warnock was
referencing is well and truly a thing of the past.

Non contact future

Old-style hard men haven't entirely disappeared from the
scene, but they are an endangered species, and no mistake.
There's Ryan Shawcross, vilified for the tackle that broke Aaron
Ramsey's ankle, and whose unfashionable style of play has
certainly deprived him of England opportunities that should
by rights have been his.

Javier Mascherano kicked the driver of one of those golf bug-
gies with a stretcher on it, while Patrice Evra kung-fu-kicked a
supporter, which seems rather a retro thing to do, doesn't it?
There's still Andy 'Elbows' Carroll, just a few years ago an international regular and one of the most sought-after and expensive strikers around. Of course he's had injury problems, but
even when fit his reputation suffers from a nagging sense that
he is just out of date.

And maybe there's also a case to be made for Diego Costa,
the cross-eyed cry-baby pirate.

But every time Alan Shearer takes us frame by frame through
an incident to show us how the goalkeeper's fingernail made
'contact' – definite 'contact' even – with some striker's trailing
sock tie, I feel the very soul of the game die a little death.

If it goes much further down this road, pretty soon FIFA
(the evil empire once presided over by Sepp Blatter) will be
in charge of a game that looks just like FIFA (the anodyne
computer game).

On
Tiki-Taka

First there was Total Football, the fluid attacking system based on pressing, possession and movement practised by the Ajax and Dutch teams of the 1970s. Then, three decades later, there was Tiki-taka, a fluid attacking system based on pressing, possession and movement, pioneered by Barcelona manager Johan Cruyff, Total Football's most brilliant exponent. As if to emphasise its roots in the 1970s, the phrase 'tiki-taka' itself comes from the Spanish name for the popular but frankly dangerous toy of that decade that we used to call 'clackers'.

Cruyff began to implement a passing and possession-based style at Barcelona, which was promoted all the way through their youth systems by subsequent Dutch managers Louis van Gaal and Frank Rijkaard, with the result that the La Masia youth academy churned out a whole generation of technically talented players with excellent touch. Many of these were physically on the small side, players such as Xavi, Andres Iniesta, Pedro, Cesc Fabregas and the Argentine Lionel Messi.

Spain began to reap the benefits as Barcelona developed this style in their first team, and the term 'tiki-taka' was first coined during the 2006 World Cup – not altogether in a complimentary way. Luis Aragones, the Spain coach, was concerned about his defence, and used possession football and an offside trap to protect a weak defence. This plan came unstuck against France, who allowed a midfield of Xavi, Fabregas and Xabi Alonso to dominate with 61 percent of play, but still broke through three times to knock them out.

By Euro 2008, however, Aragones' tactic was more refined. Spain swept all before them on the way to winning the tournament. Their midfield of Xavi, Iniesta, Fabregas and Marcos Senna was supreme, and striker David Villa was the top scorer. Now every team in Europe wanted to concentrate on ball retention.

Pep Guardiola managed Barcelona from 2008 to 2012, and 'tiki-taka' reached new heights under his regime. Typically they would overload the midfield to control possession. They counter-attacked rarely, even turning down the chance of quick breakaways by holding play up to allow team mates to get alongside and keep possession in central areas. It could be more than a little frustrating to watch.

When they were on top, though – which was most of the time – Barcelona were certainly an attacking side. And they had Lionel Messi to unlock the opposition defences. In 2009 they won a sextuple – league, cup, Champions League, UEFA Super Cup, Spanish Super Cup, and FIFA Club World Cup – which is impressive however you cut it.

Spain gradually turned ball possession into a more cautious and defensive tactic, using it to stifle dangerous opponents. When they won the 2010 World Cup they only scored eight goals in their seven matches, keeping clean sheets in all four of the knockout games.

By Euro 2012 there was somewhat less admiration, even though Spain became the first country to win three major tournaments in a row. Where the victories of 2008 and 2010 had thrilled, tiki-taka was now starting to be seen as sterile, tedious and conservative. It seemed to become more and more about preventing the opposition from scoring – after all, they couldn't hurt you if they couldn't get the ball off you, right?

Defenders who were clearly comfortable on the ball were making short safe passes into the midfield, where the rotations would begin all over again. Midfielders anxious to retain possession above all else would rarely risk a less-than-certain through ball option.

Opposition teams got to know the sort of through ball that Spain were looking for, and learned to block them off. It went from being a tactic to attack and win games, and it developed into one designed above all not to lose.

In November 2012 there was an evening of great satisfaction for those who had come to despise possession football for its own sake. Barcelona went to Celtic Park for a Champions League group game, had 83.6 percent of the possession, made 955 passes to Celtic's 166 – and lost 2-1. It was fabulous.

Pep Guardiola himself came to detest it. 'Tiki-taka is a load of s**t – a made-up term,' he said. 'It means passing the ball for the sake of passing, with no real aim or aggression – nothing. I will not allow my brilliant players to fall for all that rubbish.'

I think he's got a point. Spain's success led to a glorification of possession above all else which provided some deathly games for the neutral, especially during the Champions League. It was fuelled by the rise of Opta statistics and the like, which had been around since the mid-1990s, but began to be able to provide real-time data during matches in 2005-06.

Thankfully, football seems to have discovered the antidote. Bayern Munich beat Barcelona 4-0 and 3-0 in the 2012-13 Champions League, shutting them down with a compact midfield and using 'fake pressing' to push them back without actually over-committing. Diego Simeone's Atletico Madrid were undefeated in six games against Barcelona the following season by packing their midfield with the strikers coming deep and full backs pushing on.

In the 2014 World Cup Louis van Gaal, instrumental in the development of Xavi and Iniesta while Barcelona coach, undid them with a swift counter-attacking style that brought a 5-1 win for his Netherlands team, Spain's worst defeat for 64 years. Rattled, they lost to Chile as well and went out in the group stage.

They were favourites in Euro 2016, but Italy outnumbered them in midfield, and they bowed out of Russia 2018 after a thrilling group stage 3-3 draw with Portugal, losing out on penalties to the hosts in the last 16.

So maybe 'tiki-taka' and slow, probing, possession football has had its day.

On
Fifa and Sepp Blatter

Towards the end of his tenure as FIFA President-for-ever-and-ever-amen, Sepp Blatter was showered with cash at a press conference in Switzerland by prankster comedian Simon Brodkin as one of his alter-egos – Jason Bent, the dim pro-footballer. He did it perfectly, and the photographs of Blatter with greenbacks swirling around his evil face, grimacing in cold malignity, haunted him as he was finally engulfed in corruption scandal after financial mismanagement scandal, and are still used today whenever he makes a statement bleating his innocence or claiming he should have won the Nobel Peace Prize.

As football moved forward through decades of expansion it badly needed a governing body that would oversee developments firmly, wisely and for the benefit of all. What it got was FIFA, a governing body that oversaw every single development for the benefit of FIFA. More specifically, for the benefit of the people who were running FIFA.

When Sepp Blatter was elected president of FIFA in 1998 it wasn't the first time he'd won an election. In 1971 he had been elected President of the World Society of Friends of Suspenders, an organisation set up to lobby women to wear stockings rather than pantyhose. He won the FIFA gig, it later turned out, by lobbying the representatives of third world countries' football associations – I say lobbying, I mean paying them $100,000.

He had been General Secretary for 17 years under the previous President, Joao Havelange, who was mighty keen for his lackey Sepp to succeed him so that there would be no proper investigation into his various corrupt practices, which included taking massive bribes from ISL, the marketing company set up by his mates that was awarded television rights for the World Cup and the Olympics. (Havelange was also a big wheel at the IOC.)

Under Havelange and Blatter, FIFA grew into a worldwide force overseeing a $250-billion-a-year international industry, with gleaming new headquarters in Zurich. It reached its corrupt tentacles into every country on Earth, and yet was accountable to no one.

Every four years FIFA would enjoy a financial bonanza that few of those countries could begin to match with their GDP. First of all there would be the rights to host the World Cup, and then there would be commercial sponsorship deals associated with that, and hugely lucrative television rights to hive off to the highest bidder. The opportunities for those FIFA executives and representatives of member countries who voted on such matters to solicit and receive bribes and kickbacks was massive, everything from the designer handbags offered by the outstandingly lame England bid for the 2018 World Cup to the $1.5 million bribes allegedly paid to African executive committee voters by the Qatari bid for the 2022 beanfest.

It wasn't just the bids themselves that were hugely lucrative.

It appeared that every time a World Cup was awarded, the host country would be required to promise to construct a number of new stadia and embark on various new infrastructure projects. The contracts to build these white elephants were also highly sought after and thus a source for more potential kickbacks for the unaccountable regime.

According to the Dutch government (who refused to do this) FIFA required host bidding nations to agree to implement special laws for the World Cup, including tax exemptions for FIFA and its sponsors, and limiting workers' rights.

Over his nearly two decades in charge, Blatter became a familiar figure to football watchers. He liked to participate in draws, he liked to glad-hand with heads of state, whom he seemed to regard as his equals. He liked to hand out prizes and trophies, his lizardy-tongue flicking out to the side as he took centre stage, and he liked to do the thing of holding them up for applause which is rightly the preserve of the winner.

He would brag about FIFA's many projects around the world, his mission to spread what was already the most popular sport on the globe without his assistance. Every year FIFA would disburse huge sums in 'development-related expenses', none of which were particularly monitored or accounted for, and which seemed primarily to create large numbers of grateful football associations would happily vote for Blatter to keep the cash coming. Indeed, it came to seem as though the very purpose of FIFA's activities was merely to keep Sepp Blatter in charge of it.

But what did Sepp really do for football during his time at FIFA? Well, he held up the introduction of technology for as long as possible, until the Frank Lampard no-goal in South Africa embarrassed him into finally moving forward.

He spoke out in favour of women footballers wearing tighter

shorts, hot pants, even, his nasty little tongue flicking out as he thought (I speculate) about stockings and suspenders or groping Hope Solo, the American football star.

He interrupted a minute's silence for the recently-departed Nelson Mandela after eleven seconds because he wanted to get on with his speech.

A bargain for a salary (kickbacks not included) of $3.76 million a year, I'm sure you'll agree.

Of course there were allegations of financial shenanigans, of corruption, of bribery, but who was going to investigate these? Every time Blatter would deny all knowledge, act shocked, and refer the matter to FIFA's own ethics committee. Occasionally he would throw someone under the bus, and usually this would be someone who had stood against him for election, like an old-style Soviet purge.

It seemed as though we would never be rid of the toad. Blatter contrived to stand unopposed for election in 2011 by having his only rival investigated and by promising not to stand again in 2015. Then he stood in 2015.

Before that, though, in 2010, had been the process for allocating the 2018 and 2022 World Cups. Ordinarily FIFA wouldn't do two at once, but Blatter was anxious to dip his snout in the kickback trough as soon as possible and didn't want to wait. England were bidding, of course, and put up a 'dream team' of David Cameron, David Beckham and Prince William to plead our cause. The three men had much in common, of course – Prince William is an Aston Villa fan, Becks was offered to Villa by Sven in the 'fake sheikh' incident that led to his downfall, and Cameron was apparently a Villa fan except when he claimed to be a West Ham fan in a speech, confused by the fact that their shirts were the same colour. As his own face.

The F.A. chairman at the time, Lord Triesman, alleged that four members of FIFA's executive committee asked for bribes to vote for England's bid. FIFA dismissed this, naturally, but the four members named were among those later extricated from the Hotel Baur du Lac with sheets over their heads by the US Department of Justice.

Nicolas Leoz, the chairman of CONMEBOL, asked for a knighthood. And you do kind of wonder whether Prince William couldn't have obliged, you know, had a word. Or done the deed himself with the handle of a mop or something. Oh yes, and Leoz wanted the F.A. Cup named after him as well.

There was a general assumption that the World Cups had simply been sold to Russia and Qatar respectively. England's bid had Goldenballs, a splash of royal glamour, and the bloke who went on to cock up the whole Brexit thing in the most spectacular misjudgement in recent political history. Russia and Qatar had something more important – oil. And oil means oodles of cash, and enough of that passed beneath executive committee tables and into executive committee back pockets to seal the deal. Also, Vladimir Putin suggested that Sepp Blatter should be awarded the Nobel Peace Prize.

Qatar's bid was laughably impractical. The temperatures there in World Cup season are off the scale, and far from conducive to top-class athletic performance, let alone to health. Their ludicrous proposal contained assurances that all stadia would be air-conditioned (how?), and floated the idea that mechanical clouds could be employed to block out the sun.

This obvious fix sent rumours of corruption through the roof. FIFA responded by commissioning a report into itself, which it subsequently refused to release to the world, allowing people only to hear a positive summary of it by someone who'd read it.

In the meantime Blatter carried on serenely as ever. He backed the most extraordinary vanity project, a movie called *United Passions*, the FIFA story, which starred Gerard Depardieu (as Jules Rimet) and Tim Roth (as Blatter) who should both be heartily ashamed of themselves. The Blatter character is an incorruptible hero who tries to clean up FIFA, so it's basically pure fiction. It cost $30 million, and about nine people went to see it, all of whom hated it.

There were certainly characters in and around FIFA who wouldn't have looked out of place in an off-the-wall comedy caper film. Such as 'whistleblower' Chuck Blazer, who had a suite in Trump Tower in New York for the exclusive use of his cats. Or what about the gloriously-monickered Tokyo Sexwale, who was one of the candidates to replace Blatter? Surely there would be a place for him, perhaps as the genetically-modified superbeast who would try to defeat Godzilla by fucking it to death.

In 2015 Blatter won another term as president, but then within a couple of days an investigation by the US Department of Justice finally found a way to bring accountability to FIFA, and hauled fourteen of their executives away from the luxury Swiss hotel where they had gathered for the annual congress and charged them with racketeering, wire fraud and money-laundering.

Blatter claimed to be horrified, of course, but his turn was coming. His downfall was tied to an improper payment of $1 million to Michel Platini, the president of UEFA and widely assumed to be his successor-in-waiting. He resigned, then took his resignation back and said he would stay on until his successor was chosen, but then Coca-Cola, Visa, McDonald's and Budweiser, his beloved sponsors, all issued statements saying he had to go, and his goose was cooked.

He was banned for eight years from having any involvement in football, as was Platini. This was by FIFA's ethics committee, so Blatter knows the ban is virtually worthless. He still claims to be president, since he never lost any election, and he went to Russia to try and hang out with Putin, who (for once) knew better.

Post-Blatter, is there any hope at all that FIFA might one day be a force for good and common sense in football? Well, the signs aren't great, to be honest. Blatter's successor is Gianni Infantino – again, a perfect missed-opportunity character for the FIFA film, a baby-faced mobster assassin. He brought forward the process of allocating the 2026 World Cup because 'FIFA are broke'. This went to a hilariously impractical joint bid by pretty much the whole North American continent. You could almost see Infantino's tongue hanging out at the thought of the commercial possibilities of once again doing 'business' in the world's most lucrative commercial market. And maybe Jennifer Lopez will actually score her penalty at the opening ceremony (you read it here first).

Infantino has put forward a plan to increase the size of the finals tournament to 48 teams, which means it will be virtually impossible not to qualify for it. Even Scotland are going to be there. And there will be plenty of countries contemplating a first World Cup visit who will gratefully wish to thank Infantino next time he comes up for re-election.

He has also announced plans for a World Club Cup, 24 teams, £100 million prize money, played in China in June, in the hope of creaming off some of UEFA's Champions League lolly. Another thing to invite bids for, another thing to milk Gazprom and Budweiser for sponsorship money for, another thing for non-footballing nations to build white-elephant one-use-only stadia for.

There was no thought that Russia might lose the 2018 tournament, even when it invaded another member country. No thought, either, that Qatar might be stripped of the 2022 extravaganza, despite the construction workers who have died, and the fact that the bid is now more or less acknowledged to have been won by outright bribery. No, what we'll do instead is move the whole thing to November, which will mess up just about everything in the football calendar.

Oh yes, the world game is in very safe hands. Did I say safe? I meant same.

On
Uncle Roy and Big Sam

Hodgson

England had qualified for the 2012 Euros in Poland and the Ukraine, and someone needed to be parachuted in to take them there. That someone turned out to be Roy Hodgson, who had been in the reckoning before, only to have had a bad season at just the wrong moment. His record was good, and he was one of the few English managers who'd coached abroad, in Sweden and Italy.

Almost his first order of business was to pick John Terry for the squad and leave out Rio Ferdinand, ostensibly for 'footballing reasons', but surely to avoid friction between the pair on account of Terry's upcoming court case. And if it was that, why pick that side of the argument? This was an uncomfortable start, especially when injuries left Roy looking for a replacement centre back and he went for Martin Kelly rather than Rio.

Despite this, Hodgson went to Euro 2012 with a good deal of goodwill behind him. Expectations were low, as low as they'd been for years following the miserable dourness of the Capello regime and the demise, finally, of talk of a Golden Generation.

And so people generally were reasonably pleased with what was achieved. A Joleon Lescott header earned a point against a France side who had 19 shots to England's 3. Then there was a first ever competitive win against Sweden, 3-2, with goals from Andy Carroll, Theo Walcott and Danny Welbeck, and a 1-0 win over the co-hosts, Ukraine, thanks to a Wayne Rooney header from inches out.

In the quarter-final against Italy all the commentators and pundits creamed themselves over the passing of Andrea Pirlo as Italy had 64 percent of the possession and 35 shots to England's 9. Still, the game was goalless after extra time, and England were denied after misses by Ashleys Young and Cole.

Despite this underdog rearguard display, England found themselves ranked third in the world by FIFA after the tournament, which seemed odd, but Hodgson got on with qualifying for 2014's Brazil World Cup, qualifying ahead of Ukraine and Montenegro, and introducing the likes of Daniel Sturridge and Andros Townsend to the set-up.

The preparation was meticulous, with training camps at St George's Park and in Miami, before settling at the best facilities in Rio de Janeiro. The F.A. entourage included a psychiatrist, nutritionists, a turf specialist and cooks. The squad had individually-tailored recovery drinks after inviting scientists from Loughborough University to study their sweat patterns, and Hodgson consulted Sir Dave Brailsford, Team GB's cycling supremo, about creating a winning environment.

Yet somehow it all unravelled. Against Italy Hodgson sent out his team in an attacking 4-2-3-1 formation, with Steven Gerrard and Jordan Henderson behind a front four of Wayne Rooney, Raheem Sterling, Danny Welbeck and Daniel Sturridge. They looked a vibrant, menacing unit, with exciting movement and good use of the ball, epitomised in Sturridge's terrific half-volleyed equaliser from a Rooney cross. Unfortunately they paid the price for a couple of moments of slack defending which led to Marchisio's opener then Balotelli's headed winner. It was, however, a spirited and promising performance in defeat.

Against Uruguay they were not able to repeat it, and two Luis Suarez goals with a single Wayne Rooney reply left England facing the exit after only two games. A goalless draw with Costa Rica confirmed it, and so much preparation and early promise counted for nothing.

Hodgson had enough credit to stay on for Euro 2016, although he might wish that he hadn't. He restored his reputation somewhat with an imperious qualification, winning all ten games in a group featuring Switzerland, Slovenia, Lithuania, Estonia and San Marino. He was praised for introducing a pacy attacking style, and new forward players Harry Kane, Jamie Vardy, Marcus Rashford and Dele Alli.

Once the tournament began, however, England reverted to a negative, cagey, safety-first style of play. They were ahead against Russia thanks to an Eric Dier thunderbolt of a free kick, but then conceded an injury-time equaliser. Then they needed an injury-time goal of their own to beat Wales, Joe Hart having made a mess of a Gareth Bale free kick before subs Vardy and Sturridge scored to make the final score 2-1. A 0-0 draw with Slovakia, Hodgson having made six changes, saw them through to the last 16.

There they met Iceland in Nice, and suffered what Alan Shearer described as 'the worst England performance' he had ever seen. It began with Wayne Rooney scoring an early penalty, but within 18 minutes England were behind. A long throw caused an unreasonable amount of chaos for Iceland's leveller, and then a tame half-shot squirmed under Joe Hart's outstretched left hand.

England huffed and puffed but could not blow the blue house down, often taking punts from long range, frustrated with not being able to find a way through. Belief and composure drained away before our very eyes, and it was as if decades of underachievement and neurosis all distilled into one terrible godawful performance.

A team that had marched effortlessly through qualifying just couldn't turn it round when Iceland put them into a difficult situation. No one stepped up to take the game by the scruff of the neck, no one imposed themselves. They all just seemed powerless to stop the catastrophe from happening.

In tournaments going back to Euro 2004, England have been exposed by trying to play to the prevailing fashion. They were simply not good enough technically, or experienced enough at it tactically, to play the keep-ball that the big boys seemed to be able to do. Even players who had made a name for themselves at club level by playing a high tempo, high-energy direct sort of a game started to try something else when they pulled on England shirt – started to try to play a self-consciously 'international' sort of game, and it just doesn't suit us. We end up aimlessly passing the ball across the defence in a way which pleases no one except maybe Louis van Gaal, who seems to like that shit.

Roy Hodgson, a decent fellow who had his successes at getting a tune out of the generation after the so-called golden one, found that any progress he had made was cast aside once England were playing at a tournament, and they reverted to anxious type.

Perhaps Fabio Capello hit the nail on the head when he said that the players simply found the England shirt 'too heavy'.

Roy left the England job with the nation at its lowest level in the FIFA rankings, twentieth, when he'd seen them third after a relatively bright Euro 2012. He deserved better than to be sent out to do a press conference knowing he was going to be sacked, and with nothing to say except 'I don't know what I'm doing here'.

Allardyce

So we'd tried foreign bosses and that hadn't worked, and we'd tried English coaches and that hadn't worked, which left what? An alien? Or the man who had always touted his own credentials with great confidence, if not the biggest head in football then certainly the biggest face, a man who chewed three to six packets of aniseed-flavoured gum per match. A man who insisted he'd get the credit he deserved if he pronounced his name Allar-dee-chay.

Sam Allardyce's name finally rose to the top of the dwindling pile, as the football world gave a collective shrug and said 'Oh go on then, why not – it's not going to get any worse, is it?'

He began by bucking the trend that new England managers would always divest themselves of a senior star player from the preceding regime, stating instead that he intended to build a team around Wayne Rooney, who most pundits thought had reached the end of a record-breaking career, and claiming that the captain 'could play anywhere'. His wild-card pick was Michail Antonio of West Ham, who didn't get on in Allardyce's first game, a World Cup qualifier away in Slovakia, which was pinched 1-0 in the 95th minute by Adam Lallana.

He didn't know it at the time, but Allardyce had just claimed

England's only 100-percent winning record as manager, because before they played again he was out.

Three weeks later the *Daily Telegraph* released footage of Allardyce telling a group of 'Asian businessmen' – presumably he thought he was safe since they were not fake sheikhs – that he could show them how to circumvent FIFA and F.A. regulations on third-party ownership of players. The story was headlined 'Football For Sale'.

I don't always agree with Alan Shearer, who has a tendency to say that players 'should've scored' when they miss a quite difficult chance or the keeper makes a creditable save, but when he said that he didn't think England could stoop any lower after the loss to Iceland, and that we were now the 'laughing stock of world football', well, he pretty much nailed it, didn't he?

On
Where We are Now

As we have established, we now live and watch football in an era when the game is awash with money. At the top end, anyway. And because all the money is rising to the top, the clubs at the bottom end are struggling more than ever. The one staple source of income that could be relied upon, which was bringing on a player and then selling him on for a handsome fee, is harder to do now than ever. The big clubs run voracious academies that hoover up all the young talent, and even if you do manage to pick one up that has slipped through the net – or, more likely, been judged to be not quite up to the grade but eager to prove Manchester City or Chelsea wrong – then you can only sell him on during transfer windows that are designed to suit the big clubs.

Meanwhile the problem for the Premier League boys is this – when everyone is filthy stinking rich, how do you get an edge? The answer to that one seems to be get yourself a billionaire owner who will be prepared to sink his (or her) own cash in to fund even bigger signings, or even brighter and more spanking new stadia.

The age of the stinking rich owner began in 2003 with the acquisition of Chelsea by Roman Abramovich. He wasn't the first wealthy foreign owner, technically, but Mohamed al-Fayed had been based in the UK for many years before he took over Fulham, so the fact that he is technically Egyptian isn't relevant.

Abramovich was a new breed of super-rich owner. He'd made his money in Russian oil, and he made it clear right from the start that he was in it to have fun, that Chelsea, basically, were a rich boy's plaything. The fans didn't seem to mind, as suddenly they were able to contemplate buying any player, getting any manger, winning any trophy. Claudio Ranieri was in charge, and got Chelsea to second place and the Champions League semi-final. This wasn't good enough to keep his job, as Roman wanted the guy who had actually won the Champions League. Jose Mourinho arrived, and so did the league title in pretty short order. Managers have come and gone with startling frequency in Roman's time, but so have all of the major trophies at one time or another.

Despite being able to see the immediate impact of a billionaire foreign owner transforming a club's fortunes, Manchester United's fans were significantly less pleased than Chelsea's when Malcolm Glazer acquired their club by leveraging £550 million of debt against it in 2005.

Some of them were so dischuffed that they decided to set up a phoenix club, F.C. United of Manchester, which has never garnered the affection or support from neutrals that AFC Wimbledon has. This may be because F.C. United seemed like a fit of pique, whereas AFC Wimbledon was born out of a genuine calamity, the old Wimbledon being moved to Milton Keynes and renamed MK Dons.

As things have turned out, the Glazer takeover hasn't been

the catastrophe United fans feared. According to *Forbes* magazine Manchester United are now the second richest sports franchise in the world, and they sit in the Glazers' portfolio alongside the Tampa Bay Buccaneers. Other American sports franchise-holders have followed. John W Henry owns Liverpool as well as the Boston Red Sox, while Stan Kroenke has added Arsenal to the Los Angeles Rams and Colorado Rapids.

Wolves have Guo Guangchang, a Chinese real estate billionaire, while Leicester have Thai billionaire Vichai Srivaddhanaprabha – so not altogether the plucky underdogs in 2016. Mind you, Stoke have Peter Coates, the bet365 guy, who's richer than most of them and it didn't save them.

Even Abramovich has to give best to Sheikh Mansour, deputy prime minister of the United Arab Emirates and the richest owner of the lot, who owns Manchester City, as well as the lookalikey franchises New York City and Melbourne City.

An indication of how these men (and women) regard their acquisitions came when Stan Kroenke bought out Alisher Usmanov's share of Arsenal for £550 million. Usmanov didn't mope at being severed from his beloved Gunners, no, he immediately started wondering which club he could buy next, possibly even contemplating going into partnership with a fellow former Arsenal billionaire, Farhad Moshiri, who left the Emirates and bought Everton. These men are players, players in a big game, and the rest of us are not even mere pawns, that would be overstating things enormously.

Fans will refer to transactions as though they have some input in them or some stake in what happens. Listen to *6-0-6* if you can bear to, and it won't be long before you hear some mouthy individual opining that 'we got a good deal' on such and such a player, or 'we spent too much' on another. What is this 'we'? You're not in the picture. You support the football team, not the bank balance. Does it give you a warm feeling to know that your foreign owner is a more balls-on-the-table negotiator than another? Is your main interest to see your club further into the black than all the rest? Or would you rather see someone score a goal?

Player power

What these rich guys want these rich guys get, and players know that. More specifically, their agents know it. And what that means is that the top players are incredibly powerful. Their wages have reached obscene levels – no, scrub that, we left obscene behind a couple of decades ago – because the agents know clubs will jump through any hoops.

Look at Neymar's mind-boggling £200 million transfer from Barcelona to Paris St Germain, arranged by his agent who is also his dad. All seemed to be going through fine, but then there were delays, and delays, and it turned out that Neymar Senior was waiting until the end of the month so that Junior would qualify for a loyalty bonus from Barcelona of twenty-something million. A loyalty bonus from the club he was abandoning. The world has gone mad.

Loan arrangers

What the rich clubs would really like is for the poor clubs to be at their disposal, at their beck and call, knowing their place and humbly acknowledging that they will never again be able to compete. They pay lip service to the idea of developing new home-grown talent, but what they really want is for the rump of the EFL to do that for them, to take a bit of responsibility, like a stressed parent wanting his kids to do a bit of washing up. 'Can't you see how hard I'm working just to keep this household in the manner to which it has become accustomed? Is it really too much to ask that you do this one thing for me?!'

So the Checkatrade Trophy – formerly trading as any number of genres of bauble, shields, cups, usually named after some kind of home improvement product, which no one in the lower leagues is really bothered about until they get within a game or two of a trip to Wembley – has been transformed into an opportunity for top clubs to give a token competitive outing or two to their reserve players, masquerading as their under-21 teams. Lower EFL clubs can grind their teeth, but even though attendances and revenues are small-to-insignificant still they cannot afford to say no.

Then there are loan deals, which are the lifebelts thrown by the Billy Zanes to the drowning Leonardo di Caprios to salve their consciences for not allowing them into the lifeboats. More and more these deals are weighted – surprise surprise – in favour of the so-called 'parent' club of the young player being farmed out to get vital competitive experience. We'll keep paying all his wages, they say, so you don't have to even pay the lad a bean. 'Woo hoo!' cries the impoverished foster parent, before discovering that this only applies as long as the player is selected to start games. If he doesn't work out and they have to drop him, then they have to start paying him. Paying him Premier League teenager wages, as well, which will likely make the unwanted parasite the highest paid (non-)performer at their club, thus cheesing off everyone else who is getting picked ahead of him.

Managerial merry-go-round

Of course, all the top clubs have foreign managers now: their owners have rich tastes, and expect caviar. Surely lower down the Premier League, though, there is room for some home-grown managers to cut their teeth and make a case for one of the big jobs? Well, not really.

There's Eddie Howe, of course, who is the exception always trotted out to prove this rule, like Leicester are offered up as proof that a little club can still win the Premier League. There is Sean Dyche, but few give him much of a chance of repeating his seventh-place finish with Burnley, not with the Europa League dragging them down.

The hyper-anxious rump of the Premier League won't take a risk, instead recycling a small cadre of 'safe pairs of hands' round and round on the managerial merry-go-round. Allardyce, Hughes, Lambert, Pardew, Moyes, Pulis, McClaren, Hodgson – every time you think 'well that's that, you've stuffed that up, you're never going to get another gig', they go and prove you wrong.

It would be nice to see an English manager win something, wouldn't it? Harry Redknapp in 2008 won the Cup with Pompey. Steve McClaren the League Cup in 2004. Howard Wilkinson the league title in 1992, the last year of pre-Premier League history, back in the dark ages when Manchester United were crap and the rest of us had some sort of a chance.

In an ideal world

You can't blame a player, or an agent, or the chairman of a club for taking advantage of a situation. You can blame those who allowed the situation to develop in the first place, those who should be administering the game on behalf of all of us.

Those who should have seen what the Bosman Ruling would lead to, for example, and should have adapted and created new guidelines so that the game would not be harmed. Those who should have seen what Murdoch's involvement would inevitably lead to, and who should have taken steps to make sure that those effects were to the benefit of the whole game.

Football is a plutocracy. Money talks, and everything else – fair play, a sense of proportion, sporting integrity, history, and even, eventually, gradually, the love of the game – walks. There are such colossal sums involved that it naturally attracts the venal, the greedy, the self-interested.

What football has always needed is a benign dictatorship, by leaders or organisations that have the game's best interests at heart. What it has had is FIFA and Sepp Blatter. UEFA and Michel Platini. The Football League and the Football Association knocking spots off one another. The Premier League looking out for itself. Agents leeching onto players and milking the game for all it is worth. Broadcasters reshaping the game to suit their own ends. No aspect of the game regarded as so sacrosanct that it can't be sold off to milk another few quid from the cash cow. Fans' unswerving loyalty regarded as a bottomless asset, to be rinsed as hard and often as possible.

Football has made itself really hard to like.

Because everyone's on the game.

May 2018

At the end of the 2017-18 season I thought I had just about reached the end of my tether with football. For years I had endured a love-hate relationship with the game. I found it impossible to like, but I couldn't tear my eyes off it.

Man City had just won the league by 19 points, a margin that neatly tallied with how far ahead of the others they were in terms of their owner's wealth. Sheikh Mansour has acquired the best manager around in Pep Guardiola, and provided him with the best players – de Bruyne, Aguero, Sterling, Mane, Silva, other Silva, Walker, Stones, Ederson, Gundogan, all of whome would walk into any other team in the league, nay in Europe. It was hard to see anything but the same again next season. Jose Mourinho was moaning, feuding with anyone who would rise to his bait, and turning out a team that picks up points with football that is barely watchable for the neutral. They were second, and would likely be so again. And so on down as the 20 teams shuffled themselves into a rough approximation of financial order, with three teams who will have changed their manager to one of the usual suspects halfway through the season destined to survive on parachute payments.

Possibly my view is soured by Oldham's relegation to League Two (the 'fourth tier', formerly trading as both Division Three and Division Four), but it's hard to see much to get excited about any more. And is there nothing football can't now be used to advertise? Once it was the fear of only being good enough to play for Accrington Stanley that fuelled kids' desire to drink milk. Then Ronaldo ball juggling on a travellator to the strains of *Mas Que Nada* was used to promote… something.

Now we have David Mitchell and Kevin Bacon, an unlikely pairing if ever there was one, discussing their new ability to share data so that Mitchell's 'daughter' can 'swap out the captain of my Fantasy League team'. Where to start dismantling the depressing cynicism of this? I give up.

Worst of all, for me, was the sense that the England team had disconnected from its support, become something that people no longer got really excited about. More and more club fans mutter about not wanting England to pick their players any more in case they get injured and it ruins their chances of finishing fourth.

People blame foreign players for coming over here and flooding our top flight, making it harder than ever for English players to break through. After all, why bother to develop a young lad if you can get a ready-made European, ready-to-go, slot-straight-in, got-a-couple-of-caps, bit-of-glamour, Paul-Merson-can't-quite-pronounce-his-name kind of a guy who can do a job for you?

It's not altogether a new excuse, though, is it? It's true that Gareth Southgate only has 34 percent of the Premier League talent to choose from, but the manager who complained that he had been to see Arsenal against Manchester City and there were only five of the 22 that he could consider was Walter Winterbottom, the manager before Alf Ramsey, and he was thwarted by all the Scots, Welsh and Irishmen coming over here, taking our jobs…

I blame the press for running England down for years – or building them up so they can knock them down – and for making the manager's position 'the impossible job'. Hounding the boss out of office became like a blood sport to them. They brought down Bobby Robson, trashed Graham Taylor, and undermined Terry Venables. They hoodwinked Sven Goran Eriksson and (thank goodness) Sam Allardyce. They ridiculed Steve McClaren and Kevin Keegan, and conducted a vendetta against Fabio Capello. Worst of all they hounded Glenn Hoddle for his sincerely-held religious beliefs. Sure those beliefs were crackers, but they had no bearing on his ability to manage an international football team, besides which if he was a Buddhist espousing those views and you sacked him he'd own you. His toppling was particularly disappointing when you read Rio Ferdinand's assertion that Hoddle was the best and most innovative of the England managers he played under in his long golden generational career. Those who came after, even – no, especially – the foreign ones, espoused a 4-4-2 with religious zeal. Sven did so because that's how he always played, and he felt he saw the light when England beat Germany 5-1 – you could win games by letting the opposition have the ball and just keeping a good shape. Fabio did so because he simply didn't have any faith that England's players would be able to handle anything more complicated.Hoddle's toppling was particularly disappointing when you read Rio Ferdinand's assertion that Hoddle was the best and most innovative of the England managers he played under in his long golden generational career. Those who came after, even – no, especially – the foreign ones, espoused a 4-4-2 with religious zeal. Sven did so because that's how he always played, and he felt he'd seen the light when England beat Germany 5-1 – you could win games by letting the opposition have the ball and just keeping a good shape. Fabio did so because he simply didn't have any faith that England's players would be able to handle anything more complicated.

After the Iceland game at Euro 2016, and the Allardyce interlude, England was at its lowest ebb. The Russia World Cup was round the corner, and it was hard to see much to get too bothered about there. Let's just have our humiliating defeat to Tunisia and our useless draw with Panama before Belgium perform the last rites.

Is what I thought.

On
Russia 2018

The Russia World Cup was controversial right from the start. FIFA's awarding of the two finals to Putin's regime and to Qatar was a key aspect of the bribery and corruption scandals that brought down Sepp Blatter and many other officials. The suspicion that Russian oiligarchs had purchased the tournament never went away, and it became increasingly clear that what Putin had in mind all along was 'sport washing', that technique whereby a dodgy regime makes itself appear more palatable by hosting a major sporting event and parading a shiny façade on the world stage.

In the eight years since the announcement was made by the lizard-tongued Blatter, a number of really rather compelling reasons for taking the thing back and giving it to someone and somewhere else emerged. There was the Russian invasion and annexation of the Crimea, part of the sovereign territory of their neighbour, Ukraine. Nothing quite like that has happened in the build-up to a World Cup hosting before. There was the time Austria was annexed by Nazi Germany in the run up to the 1938 tournament, which meant that a number of their so-called Golden Generation ended up competing for a different team to the one they had qualified with. The World Cup was not quite such a big deal back then, though. This time all eyes were on Ukraine to see if they made the cut, because how could two countries co-exist at a sportfest with such diplomatic tensions loose in the air? As it happened, Ukraine didn't make it, so that concern died down.

Then there was the nerve gas poisoning of two Russians in Salisbury. They both survived, but another person later died who may have found the bottle the poison had been kept in. The World Cup had never before been tarnished by an actual poisoning, unless you believe the conspiracy theories about German spies getting to Gordon Banks's beer in 1970. Indeed, football as a whole has never really had to cope with this as a thing, outside of that time Spurs went down with mass food poisoning, allegedly lasagne-based, before a game they had to win to make the top four (which they didn't).

Britain expelled 23 Russian diplomats in March over the incident in Salisbury, complaining to the UN that Russia had used 'a weapon so horrific that it is banned in warfare'. Theresa May employed the most severe sanction available to her, saying that no members of the Royal Family would be attending the World Cup.

There was also the strong suspicion that Russia was attempting to exert underhand influence around the world through state-organised computer hacking. They had allegedly tinkered with the American election in order to get Trump into the White House, as well as our Brexit referendum and the one about Catalan independence.

Worst of all, though, was the systemic state-sponsored doping programme that tarnished every aspect of Russian sport. Its team had been kicked out of the Winter Olympics, and almost a third of its entrants at the Rio Olympics had been barred from competing. No country had had to give back more medals over doping results, not even close. The sports minister Vitaly Mutko was heavily implicated in the scandals, which reached into Russian football; indeed, Mutko had been chairman of the Russian World Cup bid in 2010. Such had been the shame of this state doping revelation that Mutko had been removed as Sports Minister and he was now Deputy Prime Minister. That's how seriously Russia took things.

When Sepp Blatter turned up at the World Cup claiming that he was still president of FIFA – 'I was elected in 2015 for four years and I never resigned' – he was hosted by Mutko, and perhaps that was his real punishment. Vladimir Putin kept his distance, presumably so as to avoid being badgered about the Nobel Peace Prize thing all over again.

When the tournament kicked off, Putin was sitting with Gianni Infantino and the king of Saudi Arabia. One can only imagine the deathless banter about human rights issues. The Russians annihilated the Saudis by five goals to nil, and after a couple of games it emerged that the Russian players had run further and faster than any other team. The Russians refused to reveal drug test figures about their squad, and FIFA kept their counsel. Who knows, perhaps that's what Putin and Infantino had been chatting about.

VAR

There's no question that, to begin with anyway, VAR – the Video Assistant Referee – was the story of the World Cup. As the tournament got under way it became clear that players were not prepared for the sort of scrutiny that the VAR was going to subject them to, and things they would normally have got away with just by keeping a sly eye on which way the referee was looking were now going to cost them dearly.

Linesmen were told not to flag for tight offsides, so that a move could continue and a goal could be ruled out later if need be. The VAR disallowed Iran's 'equaliser' against Spain, after lengthy emotional celebrations, because of an offside that actually any half-competent linesman could have clearly seen and flagged for. It did seem a bit mean to let them play on just to see if there would be a goal they could disallow.

The VAR team were watching in a control room in Moscow, and for some reason they were wearing full referee kit, with yellow referee shirts. Why? Surely this was a job they could have done in smart casual? In pyjamas, even? You wonder whether under the desk with the telly on they were also wearing boots with studs on.

There had already been more penalties than you'd normally expect by the time England played their first game in Volgograd against Tunisia. This was once Stalingrad, by the way, site of the bloodiest battle of World War II, and England fans were warned that it would be insensitive to unfurl England flags at the war memorial there. Why? We were on the same side, weren't we? Why would it have been anything other than comradely and respectful? That was a ludicrously hyper-sensitive thing to think, wasn't it? But I digress.

Apparently Gareth Southgate's preparation had taken in a peek at how things were done in the NBA, and at corners England unveiled an approach which Glenn Hoddle was soon taking credit for having dubbed 'the Love Train', whereby the players lined up before breaking apart, so that some could block the defenders' attempts to man-mark. This led to some absurd wrestling, particularly on Harry Kane, who suffered maulings that were not so much fouls as they were sexual assaults. Nonetheless the VAR, which was supposed to eradicate this and had given penalties in earlier games, looked blithely on except when a Tunisian ran into Kyle Walker's outstretched arm and flung himself to the ground. *Then* it was a penalty.

The tidal wave of righteous indignation that would surely have ensued was suddenly dissipated when Harry Kane grabbed a most unexpected injury-time winner – didn't we always draw this sort of game? What was going on?

For a supposedly dispute-settling innovation the VAR led to more discussion of refereeing decisions than ever before. Mark 'look at me' Clattenburg was like a pig in shit, frankly, as he got to pontificate on one VAR decision after another in his unexpectedly weedy little Geordie voice. And in the group stages there were more penalties than ever before, including a couple for Harry Kane in England's second game against Panama. This, again, was precisely the sort of game England have historically always struggled in, but this time the VAR played its part in a 5-0 half time lead, and by the time England's sixth looped in off Kane's heel he was in pole position for the Golden Boot.

The VAR system was still treated with a certain amount of suspicion, but then it was used to send Germany home, proving that the pass which seemed to find the South Korean opening goal-scorer offside was in fact toe-poked through by Toni Kroos, whereupon it became the best thing since sliced bread.

In the later stages the penalties dried up as the better players wised up to the fact that there were 33 cameras watching their every move. England got another against Colombia, but later in that game the VAR picked up Jordan Henderson being head-butted under the chin and decided that the offender, Barrios, should only get a yellow card. For a headbutt.

If that was a bona fide clanger, there was worse to come in the final, when Perisic was penalised for a hand ball that he could hardly get out of the way of. On the whole, though, I think VAR can be judged a success, both in terms of the decisions it helped to make or at least correct, and in terms of the number of talking points it provided. And all those extra penalties meant that there was only one goalless draw in the whole tournament.

When the Premier League started without it having been introduced, you could hear the howls of anguish at Sky HQ. How dearly would they love to have that to bat around interminably every week?

Female commentators

Vicki Sparks became the first woman to commentate on a game at a World Cup, taking her seat alongside Martin Keown for Portugal v Morocco, prompting some unpleasant reactions on social media – which is pretty much what social media is for, it seems to me. John Terry, that notable charmer, wrote on Instagram: 'having to watch this game with no volume'. When he was pressed on this point he claimed that what he meant was that his radio wasn't working. I don't really think he thought that one through.

Meanwhile Jason Cundy had to apologise – making people apologise for stuff is the other thing that social media seems to be for – after criticising female commentators on *Good Morning Britain*, saying their voices were too high-pitched. This drew stinging criticism from Piers Morgan, who called Cundy a 'sexist pig'. My view is that if you find yourself having to apologise to Piers Morgan you should think about not going outdoors for a while.

Enio Aluko and Alex Scott popped up on pundit panels, and certainly contributed at least as much in the way of enlightenment and insight as their male colleagues. Aluko ran rings around her fellow panellists Patrice Evra and Henrik Larsson, and often seemed to be the only one of the three who had been watching the same game as the viewer. Maybe I was distracted by Evra's game attempt to carry off a big blue bow tie with a red round necked sweater, which made me think he might start juggling eggs at any moment while riding around the studio on a unicycle. Larsson was a mumbling misery throughout.

On the other channel Alex Scott received the accolade, at once validating and patronising, of having her opinions immediately recycled and claimed as his own by Philip Neville, who has clearly worked out precisely how lady footballers like to be spoken to in his day job as manager of the England women's team.

Martin Keown, meanwhile, distinguished himself by opining that anyone who was reading a book instead of watching the World Cup should 'get a life'.

Death of tiki-taka

Spain completed 1006 passes in their last 16 game against Russia, which was almost as many as their opponents had managed in all their World Cup matches put together, and yet they didn't manage a single shot on goal until the 45th minute.

This is what's so frustrating about tiki-taka. Possession stats become the measure of a team's abilities. Players become more concerned with keeping the ball than with actually doing anything with it. So it gets passed comfortably, safely, from side to side, by players who are enviably capable; but worship of possession begets excessive caution. Every football fan wants to see their team working the ball, but they also want to see them attacking the opposition penalty area, and having a pop at goal. Sometimes a speculative shot, instead of another square pass, will change the tide of a game. You have to buy a lottery ticket, that's the thing. Have a go. Spain became like a bloke who has bought 1006 scratchcards, but never gets round to scratching the silver muck off them to find out what he could have won.

Colombia, penalties

England progressed through to the knockout stage via a not-altogether-dead rubber against Belgium. Both teams rested a number of key players – frustrating for those of us who reckoned that England's best chance of a trophy was for Harry Kane to be top scorer – and it was almost as if neither side really wanted to win. The second-placed team, you see, would go into what looked like the softer half of the draw rather than the side with Brazil and France in it. Belgium won it through an Adnan Januzaj goal, which no doubt sealed his rumoured unpopularity in their camp.

In the last 16 we were up against Group H winners Colombia, a tricky sort of a proposition. That Harry Kane penalty when the Love Train became the Sex Pest Express had Southgate's men seemingly in control, but Colombia's Yerry Mina bounced a late late header over Kieran Trippier's head on the goal line, and we were into extra time. Penalties drew near with the grim inevitability of a slow-motion car crash, the low hum of panic impossible to ignore.

The mind's eye returned to poor Stuart Pearce, blood draining from his face. To Chris Waddle, slumped shoulders, comforted by Lothar Matthaus. To Gareth Southgate himself, never looking like he was going to kick it hard enough. To Paul Ince, and David Batty's little skip and jump as he tried to will the ball home. To Beckham blaming the turf, and Darius Vassell, and late sub penalty specialist Jamie Carragher, and Frank Lampard and the two Ashleys.

Surely it couldn't happen again, could it? What would that do to Gareth? It was unthinkable. And yet here we were, with Jordan Henderson telegraphing his kick to the keeper's left, needing a miracle...

But then, glorious! Colombia cracked! Uribe hit the bar, and Bacca lifted his shot to where Jordan Pickford could swat it away left handed, leaving Eric Dier with the chance to win a World Cup shootout for England for the very first time. Low to the keeper's right he went, and it was there. For once it was England's players swarming from the halfway line huddle and piling on top of one another, expressions that mixed wild glee with disbelief lighting up their faces. Gareth pumped his fists and roared at the sky, having done what he needed to do to prepare his lads to swerve the nightmare that befell him twenty-two years before.

You could see the belief coursing through the team, and it oozed out of the screen, into the living rooms of the nation, and energised the whole country. Suddenly we had a team to be proud of again. They may not have been the most technically gifted, but at least they had a backbone, they weren't going to crumble like previous generations, however golden they may or may not have been.

It's Coming Home

England were in the quarter-finals, they had won a penalty

shootout, the curse was broken and anything was possible. Now the earworm began in earnest. It's coming home! Suddenly everyone was saying it, singing it. Alan Shearer said it so often, in answer to so many different questions from Gary Lineker, that it became a shearworm.

It made me anxious, all the 'It's coming home!' People texting into the BBC, or Twittering things like 'I'm so-o-o-o-o nervous! It's Coming Home!!!'

That's the problem with a World Cup campaign like this taking off. It's great that Southgate's England managed to fire up an enthusiasm for the national team that we hadn't seen, probably, since Euro 2004, but it does mean that there are people jumping on the bandwagon who don't know how to behave.

To clarify: don't say 'It's Coming Home!' as though you think that means we're definitely going to win the thing. That's not what you do. But they don't understand what they are doing wrong. Look at Prince Harry, on a jolly with Meghan in Ireland (because the Royals weren't allowed to visit Putin's Russia): 'Yah, it's *definitely* coming home.'

ITV put together a ghastly sequence of celebrities – Dominic West, Simon Cowell, Ian Poulter, Louis Tomlinson, Joanna Lumley, Jonny Wilkinson, Anthony Joshua – all repeating the mantra, which made me feel faintly ill with worry at all the fate tempting.

Unless you have invested a lifetime in it, a lifetime of disappointment, a lifetime of coming to terms, you can't really get it. We're talking about people who will shrug after England go out on penalties. Who have 'Oh well, it's just a game' as a place for their minds to go to. Fortunate people, in many ways. People who will, like the two security guards at the end of *The Truman Show*, when the entertainment that has absorbed them for so long is finally over, turn to one another and say: 'What else is on?'

Baddiel and Skinner did get it. Their song was a perfectly-pitched anthem back in 1996. A large part of the 'It's coming home' refrain was simply referring to the fact that the tournament was taking place in England, not an expectation that the trophy was coming home, or even arrogantly asserting that England was the trophy's home. But those distinctions didn't really matter, and the earworm made it to the top of the charts for the fourth time. The fact that there wasn't a new song for this campaign only served to highlight how low expectations had been at the off.

For me, the rampant outbreak of 'It's Coming Home!' was what made me begin to suspect that it wasn't.

The semi-final

England's progress to the last four was almost embarrassingly serene. Sweden, a side we'd found it nigh on impossible to beat for decades, were eased aside with goals from Harry 'Slabhead' Maguire and Dele Alli. Now Croatia stood between England and the World Cup final. Who would have thought that a month earlier?

My son was late back home, so I'd had the game on pause for five minutes. As he came through the front door we heard a massive cheer go up all up and down the street outside. Sure enough five minutes later we saw Kieran Trippier swing a twenty yard free kick into the top corner. His first international goal, and the cherry on the cake of a massively impressive campaign for him. At half time you couldn't see England losing. Kane had gone close to scoring a second, and Stones and Maguire looked like scoring every time we had a set piece.

In the second half, though, Croatia came back into it. They found reserves of strength and energy that belied the effort they had put into gruelling knockout games that had gone to extra time, and their equaliser began to look inevitable. Perisic nipped in front of Kyle Walker to score, and in extra time Mandzukic beat John Stones to the punch to nick it.

Mandzukic then spent half of the remaining eleven minutes on the ground feigning injury, and England were never able to get up a head of steam. When will VAR do something about that?

At least it wasn't penalties, that's all I could think, as the numbness began to set in. Once a little time had passed I began to realise what a remarkable thing had happened. England had ridden their luck, for once, rather than being crushed by it. They had shown a mental strength that had elevated them above their middle-range ability, and players whose reputations had been a little patchy, maybe, had made themselves into household names.

Jordan Pickford, for one. Relegated one season, then bought by a club that sacked two managers the next, he became an agile, strong, game-saving, penalty saving superstar. Harry Maguire, courageous in the air and surging forward on the deck. He had more touches in the opposition area than any other defender in the tournament, and the joint-most headed attempts on goal. Kieran Trippier created more goal-scoring chances than any other player, more than de Bruyne, Neymar, Modric, Hazard and Coutinho, who were the next best. And Harry Kane walked off with the Golden Boot, a feat achieved by only one other Englishman, Gary Lineker. So what if half his goals were penalties and one of them hit him by accident? It's a win.

Player of the tournament

At first it looked like it might be one of the usual suspects. Cristiano Ronaldo pulled off a brilliant hat trick in Portugal's opening 3-3 draw with deadly rivals Spain. He topped that off by pinging in an inch-perfect last-gasp free kick, along the way creating an unwanted brain worm as he pulled his shorts right up as if to dazzle the Spanish keeper David de Gea with the floodlights gleaming off his oiled quads. The fact that he had failed with all 45 of his previous dead ball attempts for his country only added to the moment.

He notched again in the next game against Morocco and seemed likely to be in the mix for the Golden Boot, but then his performance tailed off in the final group game against Iran, in which his old nemesis Carlos Quieroz was fuierioz when VAR failed to award his bitter rival a red card for an elbow in the face of his marker, claiming that it would have been an early bath for anyone else. And he may well have a point, because one thing VAR does is it gives the referee precious thinking time, crucial seconds to wonder 'do I really want to be the guy who sends off the big Ballon himself?'

By the time Portugal were dumped out by Uruguay in the round of 16, the Preening One had run out of steam in any case, despite having cultivated a goatee to stroke, pantomiming the suggestion that he is a GOAT – the greatest of all time. Muhammad Ali would probably have something to say about that, and he wouldn't have done so through the medium of facial hair either. Of all time, though? I suppose if he were to modestly reduce his claim to being the greatest in the world it might be easier to back up, but then he'd have had to grow a GITWEE on his chin, and what the hell is that when it's at home?

De Gea, by the way, had a pretty wretched World Cup,

looking unusually shaky and vulnerable as Spain stumbled out on penalties to the hosts, but that didn't stop Murdoch pundit Jamie Carragher describing him as 'de best keeper in the Waaiirld' as soon as the Premier League kicked off, as though the whole non-Sky tournament had never even occurred.

Lionel Messi, Cristiano's only rival for the Ballon d'Or for the last decade or so, also had a rather dispiriting time. Argentina hiccupped through the group games. First they lost to Croatia after a hilarious clanger from Willy Caballero, who booted a clearance straight up in the air and then stood stock still until it came down to be volleyed straight back past him, then they drew with Iceland before beating the rather unlucky Nigerians. Messi did score one quite cool goal, which the pundits creamed over out of all proportion, before he too exited at the last 16 stage as France steamrollered the team he was trying and failing to carry single handed.

The third pre-tournament golden boy was Neymar (Junior) of Brazil. Neymar Senior, his father and agent, had managed to line up no fewer than 27 corporate endorsements on top of his eye-watering £600,000 a week from Paris St Germain – more even than Alexis Sanchez, recipient of the Premier League's bulkiest weekly pay packet. You can wear Neymar underwear, Neymar jeans, listen to Neymar headphones as you drink Neymar-endorsed Red Bull, Pilao coffee or Prohibida beer, travel on Neymar-endorsed airlines or courtesy of Neymar's brand of car batteries. You can read Neymar's comic adventures or play with Neymar Mattel toys, and pay for all of the above with your Neymar Mastercard, perhaps spending some of the money you have accrued thanks to Neymar's favourite real estate developers.

Perhaps the most appropriate knick-knack of all, though, would be a Neymar timepiece from Gaga Milano with its diamond-encrusted number 10, which you could use to tot up the astonishing amount of time he spent on his backside at this tournament, or rolling around on the floor clutching some part of his precious anatomy. Over fourteen minutes in the first four games, which included no less than five and a half minutes against Serbia alone. Maybe there'd be some Neymar tissues with which to cry along with him, or a Neymar calculator to help you keep track of all the shots he essayed, whilst only scoring with two. He let himself down, frankly, and his country too.

You could make more of a case, probably, for Eden Hazard, the star performer of the Belgium team that knocked Brazil out. But without question the break-out performer of this World Cup was Kylian Mbappé, the French teenage prodigy. He wasn't exactly a secret, having already moved from Monaco to Paris St Germain for 180 million Euros, a fee second only to Neymar's, but he was a revelation nonetheless. The speed with which he ran away from the desperate Argentine defence was astonishing, and he became the second teenager (after Pelé) to score two goals in a World Cup game, and also the second teenager (also after Pelé) to score in a World Cup final. As if that was not noteworthy enough he refused to take a fee for playing for his country, donating the money to charity, as England's players do by the way – which ought to be enough to make Neymar Senior, at least, spit out his caipirinha – and he was named Best Young Player of the Tournament. Best Player went to Luca Modric, who was fine and scored one really good goal, but whoever thought he was more impressive than Mbappé wants his bloody eyes testing.

Aftermath

Once the final was over, with France deserving winners, the assembled dignitaries gathered on the pitch for the presentations. Suddenly the heavens opened and the place was instantly drenched by a torrential downpour. Through it all Vladimir Putin stood, half-smiling, absolutely bone dry beneath the one umbrella that his security detail had whipped out at the first hint of moisture. Next to him Emmanuel Macron stood like a drowned rat, his shirt soaked to transparency, while the poor Croatian Prime Minister in her red and white chequered trouser suit glanced over hoping for a hint of gallantry. But Putin wasn't sharing.

He was all for taking the credit, though. After all, hadn't it been a fantastic tournament, with none of the threatened crowd trouble? (The suspicion that all the hooligans had been rounded up and shipped to Siberia was very strong.)

At his next engagement, a joint press conference in Helsinki with Donald Trump, Putin accepted some obsequious congratulations and presented the American president with a football, which Trump promptly threw in the general direction of his wife, letting it bounce away down the aisle. It was a strange moment – Putin had had a triumph, but Trump just didn't understand it.

For me it was an awesome World Cup, and the first one since Italia 90 where the thrills outweighed the disappointment. It made me wonder what was next… Well, it looks like the UEFA Nations League, a godawful concoction that is part a tournament in its own right and part qualification for the baffling next Euros in 2020, which are going to be happening all over Europe with the climax at Wembley.

Actually, I can't wait.

On
The Future

Gareth Southgate's squad for Russia 2018 was the least experienced England has put together for any tournament since 2000, and more than likely for any before that too (2000 is as far back as detailed statistical breakdowns are available). In the two years leading up to Russia 2018 England's squad players averaged just 25 games a season in league and Champions League.

Partly this is the old chestnut about the ever-increasingly cosmopolitan nature of the Premier League, and the English players being squeezed out by players from around the globe attracted by the dazzlingly out-of-control wages on offer. In 1992 English footballers played 69 percent of all minutes played in the Premier League, whereas nowadays it's just 34 percent. This is behind all the countries which host the other top leagues. For example, Spanish players play 58 percent of minutes in La Liga and Germans clock up 45 percent of Bundesliga match time.

This dwindling of top-level experience for English players is exacerbated by their cultural reluctance to pursue careers abroad. In a way, why would they, given the riches on offer in England? But so many French, Spanish, Italian, German and Dutch players ply their trade in the Premier League and elsewhere that it is no surprise that England has been lagging behind in terms of the big match experience its managers have been able to call upon.

Incredibly – particularly for those of us who have watched the FA bumble myopically around for decades – the success of Southgate's squad in Russia was not achieved despite this apparent handicap – or not only despite it, anyway – but because the powers-that-be actually decided to do something about it, something that actually worked. They took the decision to make youth and age group teams into a pipeline for developing a cohesive squad with an established tactical system and a winning mentality. Effectively this would help to narrow the experience gap between England and their rivals by ensuring that young players promoted through the England set-up would have played in top level age group tournaments, ideally with success in those. Which seems to be what has been happening, even as the first team was crashing out of the World Cup in 2014 and Euro 2016, and taking a brief step back into the Stone Age during Sam Allardyce's mercifully brief tenure.

Gareth Southgate has been heavily involved in developing this approach, and he reaped its earliest rewards in Russia. The FA decided to call it this: England DNA. As you can perhaps imagine, this caught my eye. In our house, 'England DNA' will bring you flat feet, wonky teeth and a temperamental disposition to slag things off.

Apparently 'England DNA' was not the first choice of name, that was 'England Winning', but they thought people would just laugh, as indeed I did when I envisaged the marketing folk proposing that one. The core idea of 'England DNA' – which is just as funny as 'England Winning', in my humble opinion – was to get England's youth teams to play a progressive passing style of game which would then carry on through into the seniors. It reduced tactical input to a couple of strong ideas, because after all the national coaches would only have intermittent access to get the message across. Dominating the ball, making the most of set pieces, playing dynamically with consistency and confidence – sounds easy and difficult at the same time, somehow, doesn't it?

The English are not the first to try this sort of top-to-bottom overhaul, of course. We have long been envious of the French approach at their national coaching academy in Clairefontaine, which first brought them international success in 1998 and 2000 and has kept them a world force ever since. The Germans, too, responded to their humiliating performance at Euro 2000 – where they lost to England, that's how humiliating it was – by spending tens of millions of Euros each year on training grassroots coaches. The national team revived, and started receiving rave reviews for its young attackers, which led in turn to German clubs having a greater readiness to put their trust in home-grown young players, and they won the World Cup in 2014. They seem to have clung onto some of their squad for one tournament too many, judging by their frankly hilarious ejection from Russia at the hands of South Korea and Mexico, but the infrastructure is there for them to come strongly again with a new generation. As it is, almost miraculously, for England.

Last year England won the under-20 World Cup, the under-17 World Cup and the under-19 European Championship. By any measure England DNA is ahead of schedule, and producing at the very least more joined-up thinking than ever before.

The full squad can now call on players with more under-21

experience than any before, and that age group experience is beginning to encompass a good deal of actual tournament success, of the kind that can only help when, say, you are in the full squad at a World Cup and faced with a last-16 penalty shootout against, for the sake of argument, Colombia.

Last time England got to a World Cup semi-final the FA had already sacked the coach, arguably the best they ever employed, and replaced him with a bumbling twit who was way out of his depth. They bombed in the next Euros and failed to qualify for the next World Cup, struggling to cope with the expectations that had been generated by something of a freak peak.

This time? Well, the man in charge isn't going anywhere, and he has been instrumental in revamping the entire set up in such a way that more young England players should come through, with greater confidence, greater tactical awareness, and more wins and trophies under their belts.

One small alarm went off straight after Russia, when the under-19s were obliged to defend their European Championship without a number of key players, who were all required for their top clubs' lucrative pre-season friendly tours, and they crashed out with a messy 5-0 defeat to France. Complacency? A blip?

Somehow, it does seem for once like they might actually not stuff it all up, though. I feel undermined, undercut, wrong-footed. Is this what it feels like when England turn a corner and start to do things properly? Is it? I'm scared…